CW00505131

Did Jesus go to school?

and other questions about parents, children and education

Roy Peachey

redemptorist publications

Published by Redemptorist Publications
Wolf's Lane, Chawton, Hampshire, GU34 3HQ, UK
Tel. +44 (0)1420 88222, Fax +44 (0)1420 88805
Email rp@rpbooks.co.uk, www.rpbooks.co.uk

A registered charity limited by guarantee
Registered in England 3261721

Copyright © Redemptorist Publications 2019
First published June 2019

Text by Roy Peachey
Designed by Peena Lad
Cover Design by Eliana Thompson

ISBN 978-0-85231-552-1

All rights reserved. No part of this publication may be reproduced, stored in a retrieval system, or transmitted in any form or by any means, electronic, mechanical, photocopying, recording or otherwise, without prior permission in writing from Redemptorist Publications.

The moral right of the author to be identified as the author of this work has been asserted in accordance with the Copyright, Designs and Patents Act 1988.

A CIP catalogue record for this book is available from the British Library

The publisher gratefully acknowledges permission to use the following copyright material:

Excerpts from THE JERUSALEM BIBLE, copyright © 1974, 1989 by Darton, Longman & Todd, Ltd and Doubleday, a division of Random House, Inc. Reprinted by permission.

Excerpts from the New Revised Standard Version of the Bible: Anglisied Edition, © 1989, 1995, Division of Christian Education of the National Council of the Churches of Christ in the United States of America. Used by permission. All rights reserved.

Printed by Elanders UK Ltd.

Previous book by this author:
Out of the Classroom and Into the World: how to transform Catholic education
(Brooklyn, NY: Angelico Press, 2018)

Contents

Prologue: Prayerful reading **11**

I: Parents **23**
- Why was Joseph silent? 24
- Why did it take three days for Mary and Joseph to find Jesus? 38
- Are parents gardeners or carpenters? 48

II: Children **65**
- What can we learn from the twelve-year-old Jesus? 66
- How do we become children of God? 79
- Were Adam and Eve children? 92

III: Education **107**
- Did Jesus go to school? 109
- How did Jesus teach? 121
- What can Jesus teach us about education today? 131

Epilogue: Parents, children and education: three questions or one? **147**

Dedication

For my family

Acknowledgements

I am extremely grateful to the many people who have helped me while I was working on this book, especially Giselle Nizinskyj-Beaumont, Helen Birkbeck and the Redemptorist Publications team, as well as Sara Parks, Susanna Peppiatt, Paula Mendez Perez, Andy Reed, Brian Sudlow and Paddy Thompson. Any mistakes that remain in the book are undoubtedly mine, as are the views expressed here. Above all, I want to thank my wonderful family for their love, support and patience. I dedicate this book to them.

Now on that same day two of them were going to a village called Emmaus, about seven miles from Jerusalem, and talking with each other about all these things that had happened. While they were talking and discussing, Jesus himself came near and went with them, but their eyes were kept from recognizing him. And he said to them, "What are you discussing with each other while you walk along?" They stood still, looking sad. Then one of them, whose name was Cleopas, answered him, "Are you the only stranger in Jerusalem who does not know the things that have taken place there in these days?" He asked them, "What things?" They replied, "The things about Jesus of Nazareth, who was a prophet mighty in deed and word before God and all the people, and how our chief priests and leaders handed him over to be condemned to death and crucified him. But we had hoped that he was the one to redeem Israel. Yes, and besides all this, it is now the third day since these things took place. Moreover, some women of our group astounded us. They were at the tomb early this morning, and when they did not find his body there, they came back and told us that they had indeed seen a vision of angels who said that he was alive. Some of those who were with us went to the tomb and found it just as the women had said;

but they did not see him." Then he said to them, "Oh, how foolish you are, and how slow of heart to believe all that the prophets have declared! Was it not necessary that the Messiah should suffer these things and then enter into his glory?" Then beginning with Moses and all the prophets, he interpreted to them the things about himself in all the scriptures.

As they came near the village to which they were going, he walked ahead as if he were going on. But they urged him strongly, saying, "Stay with us, because it is almost evening and the day is now nearly over." So he went in to stay with them. When he was at the table with them, he took bread, blessed and broke it, and gave it to them. Then their eyes were opened, and they recognized him; and he vanished from their sight. They said to each other, "Were not our hearts burning within us while he was talking to us on the road, while he was opening the scriptures to us?" That same hour they got up and returned to Jerusalem; and they found the eleven and their companions gathered together. They were saying, "The Lord has risen indeed, and he has appeared to Simon!" Then they told what had happened on the road, and how he had been made known to them in the breaking of the bread.

Luke 24:13-35

Prologue

Prayerful reading

Of all the mysteries in the world, possibly the greatest (to me, at least) is what happens under a car's bonnet. In fact, if I am being honest, most parts of my car are a mystery to me, which is why I stick to driving and leave the technicalities to others, notably garage mechanics and my wife.

There are times, however, when the keepers of the mysteries cannot be summoned. On Christmas Day last year, for example, when I drove my car over the metal dragon's teeth that had been placed at the entrance of a local car park to encourage traffic to flow in an orderly direction. Sadly, the car park's owners hadn't counted on drivers like me. Trying to reverse out of my parking bay, I burst a tyre and was stranded. With my own lack of technical competence cruelly revealed, there was only one option open to me, a desperate measure in a desperate situation: I turned to the car's instruction manual and thought about changing the wheel myself.

We sometimes treat the Bible like a car's instruction manual. It sits in the domestic equivalent of the glove compartment and is pulled out only at times of great need, a last resort when something breaks down in our lives. It's no surprise that we struggle to find our way around it. Colossians, is that somewhere near Philippians? (Is "How to Change a Tyre" near "How to Check the Oil"?) Ecclesiastes, is that the same as Ecclesiasticus? (The carburettor, is that the same as the catalytic convertor?) And, when we find the right page, we look for clear, utterly unambiguous instructions. Should I send my child to the local Catholic school or not? (Is the knob that unlocks the bonnet under the passenger seat or by the driver's door?) Unless we are told exactly what to do, we throw up our hands and retreat into the safety of theological (or mechanical) ignorance. If the Bible doesn't tell me exactly how I should bring up my children then what choice do I have but to insist that they do exactly what I say and hope that will work? (If the manual doesn't tell me exactly how to jack up my car and change the wheel, what choice do I have but to get on the phone and insist that someone do it for me, even if it is Christmas Day?) Or maybe we treat the Bible as if it were a low-tech version of Google that can be checked whenever we need a quick answer to an ephemeral problem, but the Bible is neither a car instruction manual nor a search engine. We don't read the Bible for information or to be told what to do. We read it in order to encounter God.

Encountering God

The disciples on the road to Emmaus wanted to make sense of events they could not understand, but instead of an explanation they had an encounter. An encounter with Christ himself on the road, in the breaking of bread and in the scriptures (for their hearts burned within them as "he interpreted to them the things about himself in all the scriptures"). What they experienced was not a distant historical event but an encounter with a living person, a person who is still alive and ready for further encounters today. "Being Christian is not the result of an ethical choice or a lofty idea, but the encounter with an event, a person, which gives life a new horizon and a decisive direction", as Pope Benedict XVI reminded us in *Deus Caritas Est* ("God is Love").[1]

As beautiful as it is in its own way, you can't have an encounter with a Volkswagen engine, and you certainly can't have an encounter with a VW Polo instruction manual. A handbook may answer (some of) our questions, but it is incapable of posing any. There is no give and take with an instruction manual. What happened on the way to Emmaus, by contrast, began with a series of questions. First from Jesus ("What are you discussing with each other while you walk along?"). Then from Cleopas ("Are you the only visitor to Jerusalem who does not know the things that have happened there in these days?"). And then from Jesus again ("What things?"). In other words, there was a dialogue, and surely one of the most astounding ideas in Christianity is that "[t]he novelty of biblical revelation consists in the fact that God becomes known through the dialogue which he desires to have with us".[2]

The heart of Christianity is not a book but a person. The Word of God is, first and foremost, Jesus Christ: not the Bible. The disciples on their way to Emmaus discovered that Emmaus was not their destination; their destination was the man they thought they had left behind forever. They learned that the sacred scriptures are sacred because they bear witness to Christ, and the same is true for us today. The Bible speaks to us of Christ: it is Christ who speaks to us when we read the Bible.

---

1 Benedict XVI, *Deus Caritas Est* ("God is Love"), 1.
2 Benedict XVI, *Verbum Domini* ("The Word of the Lord"), 6.

We think that our questions are important, that they take precedence, but when the disciples met Jesus on the road it was *he* who asked *them* questions because that is what happens when we have an encounter. At least, that is what happens when we encounter Christ. We find that we no longer call the shots. We cannot control the conversation. We are questioned when we thought that we were the ones doing the questioning.

That is why Pope Benedict XVI insisted that "the Christian faith is not a 'religion of the book'". The word of God cannot be restricted to words on a page, not even to words on the pages of the Bible: "the expression 'word of God'... refers to the person of Jesus Christ, the eternal Son of the Father, made man".[3] God wants us to have an encounter with him, not with a book. We read in order to start a conversation, or, even better, to resume a conversation that started before we were aware of it.

Divine reading

If reading the Bible is one way of developing our relationship with God then our reading needs to be prayerful. Prayerful reading is one way of translating the Latin phrase *lectio divina* (though it can also be translated as holy or divine reading). *Lectio divina* fell out of fashion for many years and so may now sound rather daunting but, in its essence, it is quite simple, the *Catechism of the Catholic Church* explaining that it is where "the Word of God is so read and meditated that it becomes prayer".[4]

Reading, meditation and prayer seem like very straightforward concepts but our understanding of these words has changed considerably over time. Reading for us usually means reading in silence. We would take a very

3 Benedict XVI, *Verbum Domini*, 7.
4 *Catechism of the Catholic Church*, 1177.

dim view of anyone who chose to read the latest thriller out loud on the train during the daily commute, but reading for most people until relatively recent times meant reading out loud. They would have been baffled by the notion that reading out loud is a childish stage to be dispensed with as soon as humanly possible because they knew that when we read out loud we allow the words to affect us at the deepest level of our being. In reading aloud we develop "more than a visual memory of the written words", one great writer tells us. "What results is a muscular memory of the words pronounced and an aural memory of the words heard."[5] I am currently typing in near total darkness as I wait for my younger daughter to fall asleep. I could not tell you where each letter is on the keyboard, but my fingers retain a muscular memory of the keys' respective positions that enables me to type accurately (for the most part). This muscular memory is incredibly useful but how much more valuable would an aural memory of words be, especially an aural memory of the words of scripture? With that sort of memory, we would be able to recall the words of the sacred text wherever we were and whatever we were doing. With that sort of memory, we could rid ourselves of the need for search engines.

Our memories have been atrophied but not destroyed altogether. We still have an aural memory of the Bible that comes from attending Mass regularly. Reading out loud is not restricted to children and Benedictine monks: we also hear the word of God each week in church. Why does this matter? Because "a deep impregnation with the words of Scripture… explains the extremely important phenomenon of reminiscence whereby the verbal echoes so excite the memory that a mere allusion will spontaneously evoke whole

5 Jean Leclercq, *The Love of Learning and the Desire for God: a study of monastic culture* (New York: Fordham University Press, 2016), 73.

quotations and, in turn, a scriptural phrase will suggest quite naturally allusions elsewhere in the sacred books".[6]

Reading out loud allows the words of the Bible, and thus the Word of God, to break through our defences, to get under the surface of our lives, to affect us at a fundamental level. We could, and often do, leave our reading there, but the practice of *lectio divina* encourages us to go a step further. When we meditate on what we have read – when, in other words, we give it our full attention, the attention of mind, emotions and will – we allow our whole self to be affected by the word of God. And when that happens we cannot do anything other than pray. In fact, when that happens we find that prayer has already welled up in us.

Praying like cattle

The word that several great spiritual writers have used to describe this approach to prayer is "rumination". If we want to discover how best to pray, how best to read the sacred scriptures, we need to learn from cattle.

Cows' stomachs are wonderful organs. It is sometimes said that cows have four stomachs but, strictly speaking, they have one stomach with four compartments, the first of which – the rumen – has a capacity of about 184 litres (forty-nine gallons). The rumen is "a fermentation vat *par excellence*".[7] It is ruthlessly efficient in breaking down the hemicellulose and cellulose in grasses, shrubs and animal feed. The cow's rumen is an impressive anaerobic environment that produces not only volatile fatty acids but also huge amounts of carbon dioxide and methane (somewhere between eight and thirteen gallons per hour), which are expelled via a

---

6 Leclercq, *Love of Learning*, 73.

7 V.R. Kasaralikar, N.A. Patil, K. Ravikanth, A. Thakur and Shivi Maini, "Clinico-therapeutic evaluation of Ruchamax and Ruchamax-N in various digestive disorders and restoration of normal ruminal function", *International Journal of Phytopharmacy*, Vol. 4 (2), (Mar-Apr 2014), 67.

prodigious amount of silent belching or eructation, to use the technical term.

More relevant for anyone who wants to learn to pray more effectively is the process of rumination, or cud-chewing. Cows regurgitate the food they have eaten from the second compartment of their stomach – the reticulum – and chew it again to break it down into a manageable size. Squeezing out fluid from the bolus of partially digested material with their tongue, they reswallow it (to give the third compartment of the stomach something to do), and then, after a lot more chewing, they swallow the cud, allowing it to be digested in the fourth of their stomach compartments. All in all, it is an impressive way of breaking down huge amounts of life-giving material. *Lectio divina* begins with reading the words of scripture aloud, which slows us down and allows those words to penetrate to a deep level. Ruminating works in a similar way. Chewing the cud is a way of getting all the goodness out of the initial feed over an extended period of time. Rechewing what has already been swallowed is the essence of rumination. We can return again and again to what may have been a few minutes of reading snatched from a busy day. We are not obliged to digest our spiritual reading immediately, but can chew, swallow and then chew again.

Time for prayer

If we were to pare it down to essentials, we could say this: in order to ruminate, all we need is something to chew on and plenty of time. The Bible provides us with plenty to chew on, so all we need to do is find time to chew. Unfortunately, the curse of our modern age is that none of us has enough time. One way of understanding the last hundred years is to see it as an era that has been dominated by the search for time-saving devices, from the car to the washing machine to thousands upon thousands of apps. We have spent a huge amount of time searching for ways of saving time and yet the reality is that many of us work longer hours than ever, our chief regret being that we do not spend enough time with our families. We become overwhelmed by emails. We lose sight of reality while absorbed in social media. Dizzied by the internet's ability to distract, we forget to graze and never quite get round to ruminating.

The great value of *lectio divina* is that it can help us to slow down, read carefully and meditate prayerfully. It can give Our Lord the opening he is always looking for. We try to block out silence with noise, but ask any cow and she will tell you that it is extremely difficult to ruminate when the TV is on in the background, when the radio is playing or when headphones are shovelling music into every available cranial space. So, if we are serious about developing a relationship with God, we need not only to read our Bibles, but also to find time, space and quiet to be able to ruminate on what we have read.

To many parents this might seem like a laughable notion. As parents, we do not have the benefits of monastic silence. Instead of the liturgy of the hours, we grab minutes where we can. In the busyness and noise of each day, *lectio divina* might well appear to be a pipe dream. Praying like cattle might well seem an impossibility when we have domestic chores, children needing our attention and a job to hold down.

The *Catechism of the Catholic Church* suggests in a very beautiful passage that it is precisely in situations like these that we can encounter God in prayer. In a section headed simply "Today", it gives this wise advice:

> We learn to pray at certain moments by hearing the Word of the Lord and sharing in his Paschal mystery, but his Spirit is offered us at all times, in the events of each day, to make prayer spring up from us. Jesus' teaching about praying to our Father is in the same vein as his teaching about providence: time is in the Father's hands; it is in the present that we encounter him, not yesterday nor tomorrow, but today: "O that *today* you would hearken to his voice! Harden not your hearts."
> Prayer in the events of each day and each moment is one of the secrets of the Kingdom revealed to "little children", to the servants of Christ, to the poor of the Beatitudes. It is right and good to pray so that the coming of the Kingdom of justice and peace may influence the march of history, but it is just as important to bring the help of prayer into humble, everyday situations; all forms of prayer can be the leaven to which the Lord compares the Kingdom.[8]

Praying in the events of each day could mean ruminating in the shower (though, admittedly, this can have serious consequences for household bills), ruminating while washing up or ruminating while having a tea break. It could also mean looking for moments of grace to open up before us at unexpected times and in unexpected ways.

It is easy to believe that if only this or that aspect of our life were different, all would be well with our spiritual life, our

8 *Catechism of the Catholic Church*, 2659-2660.

work and our parenting. However, the story of the disciples on their way to Emmaus suggests that it is precisely in the here and now, in the messiness of today, that we meet Christ. The story of the disciples leaving Jerusalem for Emmaus also reminds us that, important as the scriptures are, reading the Bible is not the only way of encountering God. We meet God in the Bible, in other people and in the breaking of bread. We meet him when we are open to an encounter. The disciples could have refused to answer Jesus' opening question, citing the need to reach Emmaus quickly as their excuse. They could have walked off in a huff when the stranger told them they were foolish, and they certainly could have avoided eating with him that evening. Instead of taking these opportunities to wriggle out of an encounter, they chose instead to listen, took the rebuke, and showed true generosity by inviting him to dine with them. Like little children, they were humble enough to allow the encounter to happen.

The story of the disciples on the road to Emmaus shows us that the essential encounter with God takes place beyond the words on the page. That is why this book takes the form it does, each chapter starting with a question that is based on one or more biblical passages but not necessarily finishing with the same question. Reading the Bible prayerfully can take us away from the concerns we begin with and lead us into some very unexpected places. That is why we need to be open to wherever God wants to take us. The story of the disciples on the road to Emmaus also reminds us who is in charge. I certainly do not claim to be an expert on parents, children or education. In fact, I am writing this book because I too am searching for answers: I want to understand my children better; I want to be a better parent; I want to make sense of education today. Even more importantly, I am searching for a daily encounter with Christ who answers our questions and poses plenty of his own as well. I have no advice to give, but I know that the mysterious man – who was God – who accompanied the disciples on the road has all the answers we need.

In the course of the book, we will look at a wide range of biblical passages but we will keep returning to those passages that touch on the hidden life of Christ in the years before he began his public ministry. It is from these passages in particular that we can seek answers to our questions about parents, children and education today. If Christ's life was hidden during those first thirty years then ours can often seem hidden too. We do not always understand ourselves. We often struggle to know how we can best raise and educate our children. We can feel overwhelmed by the daily business of life. This book is written for anyone who is still on the journey, like the disciples on the road to Emmaus, for anyone who doesn't yet have all the answers, whose life seems hidden and unimportant. By looking again at what the Word of God has to say to us today through the word of God, I hope that a new light will be shone in the darkness, in the places where our hidden lives meet the hiddenness of Christ.

I

Parents

Now every year his parents went to Jerusalem for the festival of the Passover. And when he was twelve years old, they went up as usual for the festival. When the festival was ended and they started to return, the boy Jesus stayed behind in Jerusalem, but his parents did not know it. Assuming that he was in the group of travellers, they went a day's journey. Then they started to look for him among their relatives and friends. When they did not find him, they returned to Jerusalem to search for him. After three days they found him in the temple, sitting among the teachers, listening to them and asking them questions. And all who heard him were amazed at his understanding and his answers. When his parents saw him they were astonished; and his mother said to him, "Child, why have you treated us like this? Look, your father and I have been searching for you in great anxiety." He said to them, "Why were you searching for me? Did you not know that I must be in my Father's house?" But they did not understand what he said to them. Then he went down with them and came to Nazareth, and was obedient to them. His mother treasured all these things in her heart. And Jesus increased in wisdom and in years, and in divine and human favour.

Luke 2:41-52

Why was Joseph silent?

The story of Jesus at twelve years old is one of the most intriguing vignettes in the Bible. So intriguing, in fact, that I shall return to it more than once in this book. But, for now, I want to concentrate on just one little detail in the story. After searching for three days, Jesus' parents found him in the Temple and Mary asked: "Child, why have you treated us like this? Look, your father and I have been searching for you in great anxiety." We are told Mary's words but, surprisingly, Joseph remains silent. And not just on this occasion. It may come as even more of a surprise to discover that the Gospel writers do not tell us one word that St Joseph ever said. Even when the angel came to him in a dream, he remained silent. He acted and he acted quickly, but he did not speak a word. This is in marked contrast to Mary, who accepted God's will for her with words – "Here am I, the servant of the Lord; let it be with me according to your word" (Luke 1:38) – and who responded to Elizabeth's greeting with the magnificent outpouring of praise that we know as the Magnificat.

In one of his apostolic exhortations, *Redemptoris Custos* ("Guardian of the Redeemer"), St John Paul II explained this important difference between Joseph's and Mary's responses to the word of God: "While Mary's life was the bringing to fullness of that *fiat* first spoken at the annunciation, *at the moment of Joseph's own 'annunciation'* he said nothing; instead he simply 'did as the angel of the Lord commanded him' (Mt 1:24). And *this first 'doing' became the beginning of 'Joseph's way.'* The Gospels do not record any word ever spoken by Joseph along that way. But *the silence of Joseph* has its own special eloquence".[1]

On one simple level it is clear that Joseph was a doer. Matthew tells us that, after an angel appeared to him in a dream, Joseph sprang into action and did as the angel

---

1 St John Paul II, *Redemptoris Custos* ("Guardian of the Redeemer"), 17.

commanded. In a similar way, when the angel reappeared to warn Joseph about the threat to Jesus' life from Herod, he "got up, took the child and his mother by night, and went to Egypt, and remained there until the death of Herod" (Matthew 2:14-15), at which point the angel spoke to Joseph again. For the third time, Joseph did as he was told without uttering a word of reply, or at least any word of reply that is recorded in the Gospels:

> When Herod died, an angel of the Lord suddenly appeared in a dream to Joseph in Egypt and said, "Get up, take the child and his mother, and go to the land of Israel, for those who were seeking the child's life are dead." Then Joseph got up, took the child and his mother, and went to the land of Israel. But when he heard that Archelaus was ruling over Judea in place of his father Herod, he was afraid to go there. And after being warned in a dream, he went away to the district of Galilee. There he made his home in a town called Nazareth... **Matthew 2:19-23**

Joseph was a man of action but also a man of silence. St John Paul II explained that the "same aura of silence that envelops everything else about Joseph also shrouds his work as a carpenter in the house of Nazareth. It is, however, a silence that reveals in a special way the inner portrait of the man. The Gospels speak exclusively of what Joseph 'did.' Still, they allow us to discover in his 'actions' – shrouded in silence as they are – an aura of deep contemplation. Joseph was in daily contact with the mystery 'hidden from ages past,' and which 'dwelt' under his roof. This explains, for example, why St. Teresa of Jesus, the great reformer of the Carmelites, promoted the renewal of veneration to St. Joseph in Western Christianity".[2] In other words, St Joseph was a man of action *because* he was a man of silence. Drawing from the deep well of God's goodness that was now closer than he could ever have imagined in the person of Jesus, he responded to God's special call in an utterly self-effacing way.

Silence as difficulty or liberation

St Joseph provides us with an inspiring example to follow, but even if we are inspired we may still have questions about what all this means for us today. In today's world, some people – and perhaps all of us some of the time – find silence difficult. We describe it as "stony" or "awkward" because we fear or distrust it. When silence descends we quickly fill the gap by cranking up the music, switching on the radio or starting a conversation. We associate silence with exams and Victorian schoolrooms. A pause in a sentence feels wrong if it lasts more than a second or two. When our children go quiet we assume they are up to no good.

However, though silence can be difficult, it can also be liberating. Because we are assailed by everything from car engines to the insistent beat of music from someone else's smartphone, we yearn for silent oases in the midst of our noisy days. That is why there has been a glut of films and books about silence in recent years. Patrick Shen's documentary *In Pursuit of Silence*, for example, is a clear response to a world grown loud. Taking us on a journey around the world's quiet places, from Japanese forests to an improbably silent New York bar, the film suggests that silence is not a luxury from a bygone age but an ever-present concern in our modern age. Another great film is *The Artist*, Michel Hazanavicius'

2 St John Paul II, *Redemptoris Custos*, 25.

2011 silent homage to a bygone era, which was a popular and critical success, winning five Oscars despite the fact (or, perhaps, *because of* the fact) that it celebrated the golden age of silent films. Another wonderful movie, though much less well known, is Philip Gröning's *Into Great Silence*, about the monks of the Grande Chartreuse. Gröning's film seeks to recreate the silent rhythms of the Carthusian life, leading us away from everyday noise to a place of great calmness and prayer.

And then there are the many books that promote silence, from Helen Lees' *Silence in Schools* to *Silence: In the Age of Noise* by the Norwegian explorer Erling Kagge, to Cardinal Robert Sarah's wonderful book on *The Power of Silence*. Silence, for all these writers and filmmakers, is a great force for good, a source of healing in a world gone wrong. It is neither difficult, nor awkward, nor stony.

Four ways of keeping silent

So how do we square this silent circle? How do we make sense of an absence that might also be a presence? One starting point might be to draw a distinction between outer and inner silence.[3] It is a distinction that the Bible suggests, though that may not be clear in English translation. In Greek, however, there are at least four different words that can be translated into English as "silent" or "silence". The word used when Jesus silences the Sadducees, for example, is φιμόω,[4] which means "to muzzle", a word that is also used when Jesus tells an unclean spirit to "be silent, and come out of him" (Luke 4:35). This word suggests an outer silence or an outer silencing. The heart of the Sadducees is, sadly, not changed, but they do stop challenging Jesus about the resurrection. The unclean spirit is rebuked but it is still an

3 I am indebted to Brian Sudlow for this point and for many fruitful ideas about silence.
4 Matthew 22:34.

unclean spirit. When Jesus is brought before the High Priest, by contrast, the word used for his silence is σιωπάω. Jesus does not speak but he also has an inner strength, an inner silence, that the High Priest does not understand. This is the silence that the disciples gradually develop themselves. After the transfiguration, for example, they keep their silence (Luke 9:36), with the word σιγάω being used, the same word St Paul used in his Letter to the Romans when he wrote about "the mystery that was kept secret for long ages" (Romans 16:25).

There are even more words for silence and keeping silent in the New Testament, as well as words that are closely related, the most interesting of which is ἡσυχάζω, the word St Paul uses when telling the Thessalonians "to aspire to live quietly" (1 Thessalonians 4:11). This seems like a very odd comment from someone whose own life was full of dangers and adventure! He certainly wasn't telling his readers to settle down, slip on their slippers and put their feet up by the fire. Knowing that there is a great deal more to silence than an absence of words, he was encouraging them to develop a contemplative spirit in the midst of a busy and dangerous world. This aspiration to live quietly was in stark contrast with its opposite, the disorderly (ατακτως) life, which he wrote about in his Second Letter to the Thessalonians.[5] Internal silence trumps external disorder every time, for individuals and for the community too.

Inner silence

Inner silence is built on the realisation that there is "no place on earth where God is more present than in the human heart", as Cardinal Sarah put it.[6] This is a staggering thought. So staggering that even as great a saint as Augustine of Hippo

---

5 I am indebted to Susannah Peppiatt for this point.

6 Cardinal Robert Sarah, *The Power of Silence: against the dictatorship of noise* (San Francisco: Ignatius Press, 2017), 23.

only got to grips with it comparatively late in life: "Late have I loved You, O Beauty so ancient and so new, late have I loved You!" he wrote in his *Confessions*. "For behold You were within me, and I outside; I sought You outside and in my unloveliness fell upon those lovely things that You have made. You were with me and I was not with You."[7] If God is within us, at the deepest level of our being – in what the Bible calls the heart – then the only response we can give is to remain in silence before him. The *Catechism* teaches that, "[a]ccording to Scripture, it is the *heart* that prays. If our heart is far from God, the words of prayer are in vain":

> The heart is the dwelling-place where I am, where I live; according to the Semitic or Biblical expression, the heart is the place "to which I withdraw." The heart is our hidden centre, beyond the grasp of our reason and of others; only the Spirit of God can fathom the human heart and know it fully. The heart is the place of decision, deeper than our psychic drives. It is the place of truth, where we choose life or death. It is the place of encounter, because as image of God we live in relation: it is the place of covenant.[8]

Our words and actions are as nothing compared with that stupendous realisation: God is within us. The creator of the universe has made his home in the heart of his creation. Without this inner silence that comes from the work of God within, we are unable to appreciate outer silence. Without

7 St Augustine, *Confessions* (London: Sheed & Ward, 1944), 10:27.
8 *Catechism of the Catholic Church*, 2562-2563.

this inner silence we are unable to function in the brash, noisy, contemporary world. Without this inner silence, we are unable to give our children what they truly need, which is ourselves.

Outer silence can be forced. Outer silence can signal the absence of anything worthwhile to say. Outer silence may be a sign of inner fear. There may be outer silence when we sit an exam, but that outer silence can be accompanied by inner turmoil. When a child stops communicating with his or her parents there is likely to be an outer silence that masks a great deal of inner turbulence. But inner silence is quite different. Inner silence thrives when there is outer silence but it is not dependent on it. It is (just about) possible to develop inner silence during the morning commute, in a noisy city, in a busy home or in a carpenter's workshop.

St Joseph's silence

The silence of St Joseph had nothing to do with outer silence – we can presume that his workshop was not devoid of noise – but had everything to do with a deeply rooted inner silence, an attentiveness to God who, mysteriously, had now become his own son. That is why Pope Benedict XVI, in a moving Advent Angelus reflection, was able to explain the silence of St Joseph in this way:

> His silence is steeped in contemplation of the mystery of God in an attitude of total availability to the divine desires.
>
> In other words, St Joseph's silence does not express an inner emptiness but, on the contrary, the fullness of the faith he bears in his heart and which guides his every thought and action.

It is a silence thanks to which Joseph, in unison with Mary, watches over the Word of God, known through the Sacred Scriptures, continuously comparing it with the events of the life of Jesus; a silence woven of constant prayer, a prayer of blessing of the Lord, of the adoration of his holy will and of unreserved entrustment to his providence.

It is no exaggeration to think that it was precisely from his 'father' Joseph that Jesus learned – at the human level – that steadfast interiority which is a presupposition of authentic justice, the 'superior justice' which he was one day to teach his disciples (cf. Mt 5: 20).

Let us allow ourselves to be 'filled' with St Joseph's silence! In a world that is often too noisy, that encourages neither recollection nor listening to God's voice, we are in such deep need of it. During this season of preparation for Christmas, let us cultivate inner recollection in order to welcome and cherish Jesus in our own lives.[9]

Children and silence

St Joseph has a wonderful lesson to teach parents who may sometimes find themselves at their wits' end. He reminds us just how essential it is to develop a contemplative spirit in the midst of our family life, how vital it is that we create a cloister in the world.[10] So how do we develop and maintain this inner silence? How do we help our children develop and maintain it? A useful place to start is by listening in silence. Listening

9 Benedict XVI, "Angelus Reflection", Vatican Website (18 December 2005). <https://w2.vatican.va/content/benedict-xvi/en/angelus/2005/documents/hf_ben-xvi_ang_20051218.html>, accessed 28 Dec. 2018.

10 Patrick Barry, *A Cloister in the World* (St Louis, MO: Outskirts Press, 2005).

is an underrated skill. Many of us tend to leap in rather than stand back. We can be keener to talk about ourselves than to listen to others but, as Cardinal Sarah wrote, the "silence of listening is a form of attention, a gift of self to the other, and a mark of moral generosity".[11]

What Jesus knew of carpentry, he learned from St Joseph. He also learned "steadfast interiority" from his parents, which should be an encouragement to us as we seek to learn from the Holy Family. My dad is not a carpenter but he is more practically skilled than I am, which means that I listen to him, watch him and learn from him when we are working on a task together. When I do this, I pick up a certain amount of practical know-how, but the real lesson I learn by working with him is about focus and perseverance. What I learn is what is within.

As parents, we teach our children whenever we are with them. We teach them by simply being who we are, which means that we too need to develop a sense of silent, steadfast interiority. In a fascinating talk for parents at The Heights School in Washington, DC, Andy Reed suggested three ways in which we can do this.[12] He explained that we need to be alive to the world, taking every opportunity to appreciate the beauty around us, whether it is found in nature, music or art. Then we need to slow down in order to internalise it. That is the only way, he says, that we can participate fully in beauty. In fact, he goes further by suggesting that, in the midst of our busy lives, we "have to slow down first in order to realise why [we] have to slow down". Having internalised beauty, we can then be creative with it. The example he gave was of his family listening

---

11 Cardinal Sarah, *The Power of Silence*, 81. See also Adele Faber and Elaine Mazlish, *How to Talk so Kids Will Listen and Listen so Kids Will Talk* (Dorking: Piccadilly Press, 2013), 10-11.

12 Andrew Reed, "Family: The Most Formative School", The Heights School Website (12 November 2018), <https://heights.edu/lecture/family-formative-school/>, accessed 28 Dec. 2018.

to "Gabriel's Oboe", the hauntingly beautiful theme from Ennio Morricone's score for *The Mission*, and the pleasure he gained from hearing his daughter practising it in another part of the house shortly afterwards. By attending to the beauty of the world, he argued, we begin to transform unsettled minds into quiet, creative minds.

This distinction between unsettled minds and quiet minds is a really useful one, partly because it reminds us of the fundamental importance of attention. If prayer is a relationship with God, as Simon Tugwell suggests in his wonderful book on prayer, then "one of the main problems is that half the time we just forget about it".[13] Tugwell writes about the importance of building up good habits of virtue but he is also realistic enough to point out that "just where we need to build up good habits is often precisely the occasion when we simply forget all about it. For all our beautiful meditations on forgiveness, when someone actually treads on our toe, we hit him; and only remember afterwards that we were supposed to turn the other toe over to him too".[14] One of the reasons why *lectio divina* is so important is that it helps us build up a Christian memory. Or, to put it another way, it reminds us to pay attention to God and to other people. It gets under our skin. It works its way into the silent places that are to be found at the heart of our lives and transforms us from within. "As long as our religion remains at the level of our deliberate, not to say contrived, personality," Tugwell writes, "it is bound to be a rather on-and-off affair; if we allow God to get hold of us at the level of what the Bible calls the heart, below the level of contrivance, then we have a traitor in the camp! We shall become involved with God even in spite of ourselves."[15]

---

13 Simon Tugwell, *Prayer: Living with God* (Dublin: Veritas Publications, 1974), 3.
14 Tugwell, *Prayer*, 4.
15 Tugwell, *Prayer*, 12.

And if we become involved with God then we find ourselves able to help our children become involved with God too. Just as Jesus – on the human level – learned from St Joseph's silence, so too will our children learn from our silence. As parents we are always our children's first educators, but we don't always need to teach with words.

Dog walking and prayer

Andy Reed tells the story of a father of a large family, who didn't like dogs. He was, however, in a minority of one in his family, so eventually he agreed that the family could have a dog – any dog – on one condition: he would walk it every evening as long as he could take a different child with him each time. That way, he would be able to guarantee that he was giving time to each of his children. One reason that story resonated with me is that we too have recently acquired our first dog, despite my initial reluctance but to the delight of my wife and children. I have to admit, though, that I have enjoyed the opportunity to get outside for a walk at least once a day. I have also appreciated the fact that a walk round the block is just about long enough for me to say five decades of the rosary, though I haven't yet managed to juggle dog lead, dog bag and rosary beads to my complete satisfaction. What the daily walk has given me is a clear time in which to give my attention to God. Perhaps more importantly, it has cleared a space for God to be able to get through to me. Simon Tugwell is quite right to say that if "we want to keep company with God, we must be prepared to let him remind us of his ways, not at the times that suit us, but at the times that suit him", but it is also true that setting aside regular moments of silence allows God to get a foot in our door, or maybe allows us to hear his insistent knocking that we usually drown out with our noise and busyness.[16]

16 Tugwell, *Prayer*, 14.

Of course, we don't have to bring a dog into the household to create moments of silence. There are other ways of clearing the decks. Being determined to start praying the rosary every day, I decided to keep the car radio off during my daily commute one October and found that I had just about the right amount of time to pray five decades before getting to work, unless I got caught in traffic, in which case I had the added benefit of being able to pray a decade or two more to help me through my rush-hour frustration.

Once we have started to use our dead time for silent – or near silent – prayer we may well find it difficult to stop. One priest I know measures journeys by the number of decades of the rosary he is able to pray. Guildford to Leatherhead: that's six decades. Leatherhead to Woking: that's four.[17] There is, in fact, a venerable tradition of measuring time in this way: in seventeenth-century Chile an earthquake was said to have lasted for two Credos, while it took one Ave Maria to cook an egg (which suggests that seventeenth-century Chileans must have said their Hail Marys very slowly and respectfully. Either that or they liked their eggs very runny). Parents often struggle to find silence in their lives, which is why they may collapse in a heap after the children have eventually gone to sleep, but if we are creative we can make opportunities to give God and our children the attention they deserve. That is why, having listened to Andy Reed's talk, I try to walk our dog with each of my children in turn to ensure I am giving them each some undivided attention, though I still appreciate the opportunity to take the dog on my own when it arises.

Thinking about dog walking and the daily commute does not mean that we should ignore more traditional ways of praying in silence. It would be eminently sensible to teach

17 These measurements are given purely for illustrative purposes. Please do not rely on them if you are ever planning to make these particular journeys!

our children the value of silent prayer by praying in silence before or after Mass, by popping into church when we can and by attending Eucharistic Adoration with them. And if Eucharistic Adoration is an unfamiliar practice, there are creative ways of introducing it. The Fr Leopold Lego set, for instance, comes complete with mini Lego hosts and a monstrance so children can learn the value of silent adoration through creative play. It may not have been the means St Joseph used, but that doesn't render it entirely worthless. However, we also need to hold on to the fact that teaching our children is not ultimately about finding the right techniques. What the silence of St Joseph shows us is that when we draw close to God we are bound to draw our children closer to him too. When we lay aside the noise that can daily afflict us, we can give our attention to what truly matters, which really means the one who truly matters.

Now every year his parents went to Jerusalem for the festival of the Passover. And when he was twelve years old, they went up as usual for the festival. When the festival was ended and they started to return, the boy Jesus stayed behind in Jerusalem, but his parents did not know it. Assuming that he was in the group of travellers, they went a day's journey. Then they started to look for him among their relatives and friends. When they did not find him, they returned to Jerusalem to search for him. After three days they found him in the temple. Luke 2:41-46

Why did it take three days for Mary and Joseph to find Jesus?

The story of Jesus at twelve years old is intriguing on all sorts of levels. One of the questions that might particularly strike us as modern readers is how it was possible to lose Jesus, of all people, for three days. Behind this question lie several others: how much freedom were children given at that time? Why did it take Mary and Joseph a whole day to notice his absence? And why did Jesus remain in Jerusalem in the first place? As parents, we have become increasingly aware of the dangers that our children face, with the result that we allow them very little freedom. Our parents may have had the freedom to roam around the countryside when they were young but we dare not allow our own children to do the same. And if that is true of our parents' generation, how different must the situation have been in Jesus' day?

So we have to adopt a different mindset if we are going to understand how Mary and Joseph became separated from Jesus and why it took them three days to find him. But adopting a different mindset, especially the mindset of a bygone era, is a real struggle for us today. "In an age which is so conscious of the virtue of being a good listener," Simon Tugwell writes, "it is curious how little attention is paid to the virtue of being a good listener to the voice of the Church; by which I do not mean only or even primarily the magisterium of the Church, though that is certainly not excluded, but the voice of tradition, of all our fellow Christians down the ages, stumbling and fumbling, but yet constantly returning to certain basic points, which become all the more solid and decisive for being reached from so many different angles."[18] If we are going to understand the role of parents in first-century Palestine, we must first accept that we really can

18 Tugwell, *Prayer*, 7.

learn from the past, that we haven't got everything taped, that there may be other ways of seeing things.

The power of old books

That is why it can sometimes be useful to step out of our comfort zone and read old books. Books like *On Jesus at Twelve Years Old* by St Aelred of Rievaulx. Rievaulx Abbey is now a tourist destination, its bare ruins a testament to the lasting power of Henry VIII's land grab, but in the 1150s when St Aelred was its abbot it was a thriving community, numbering some six hundred monks. Rievaulx Abbey may no longer be a going concern but St Aelred's book certainly continues to provide food for thought. In an early chapter, for example, he points out that "we must not forget that it was a Jewish custom for the men and women to go up to the feast day separately. ... And so we can understand more easily that Jesus granted his sweet presence now to His father and the company of the men, now to his mother and the women who journeyed to Jerusalem with her".[19] In those circumstances, it is not so surprising that Mary and Joseph should both have assumed that Jesus was with the other group. Blessed Columba Marmion, the Irish Abbot of the Abbey of Maredsous in Belgium, wrote something similar in the early years of the twentieth century:

> At the time of the Passover, as you will understand, the number of Jews who were in the city was very considerable; and this gave rise to crowding and congestion such as one can hardly imagine. On the return, the "caravans" – the particular sets of pilgrims who would leave together – were formed with extreme

19 St Aelred of Rievaulx, *On Jesus at Twelve Years Old* (London: Saint Austin Press, 2001), 26.

> difficulty, and it was not before well on in the day that people were able to get their bearings. Moreover, young persons could join this or that group in their caravan as they pleased; that was the custom. Mary believed that Jesus could be found with Joseph. She therefore journeyed on, singing the sacred hymns. Above all she thought of Jesus, expecting to see Him again soon.[20]

The commentaries of St Aelred and Blessed Columba Marmion point us in the direction of an answer to our question of why it should have taken Mary and Joseph three days to find Jesus. If they had been travelling for a day before noticing his absence, it must have taken them close on a day to retrace their steps. It is hardly a surprise, then, that it was only on the third day that they found him in the Temple.

There is, however, another reason why it took Mary and Joseph three days to find Jesus and that is because they did not know where to look. This truth, which is implicit in the story, is made explicit by Jesus in his response to Mary's comment that "your father and I have been searching for you in great anxiety" (Luke 2:48). He replied by asking: "Why were you searching for me? Did you not know that I must be in my Father's house?" (Luke 2:49). A great deal could be said about this response but, for now, we can limit our discussion to the question of why it had to be said at all. Since Mary had been preserved from the inheritance of original sin, we might have assumed that she would have realised straightaway where her son was. The truth was that she didn't, which is why she found Jesus only on the third day.

20 Blessed Columba Marmion, *Christ in His Mysteries* (Leominster: Gracewing, 2009), 190.

There is no contradiction, however, between her sinlessness and her ignorance of Jesus' whereabouts because Mary also "advanced in her pilgrimage of faith" during her lifetime, as the fathers of Vatican II put it.[21] She too needed to learn from her own son, which is why St John Paul II glosses the passage in this way in his encyclical on the Mother of the Redeemer, *Redemptoris Mater*:

> However, when he had been found in the Temple, and his Mother asked him, "Son, why have you treated us so?" the twelve-year-old Jesus answered: "Did you not know that I must be in my Father's house?" And the Evangelist adds: "And they (Joseph and Mary) did not understand the saying which he spoke to them" (Lk. 2:48-50). Jesus was aware that "no one knows the Son except the Father" (cf. Mt. 11:27); thus even his Mother, to whom had been revealed most completely the mystery of his divine sonship, lived in intimacy with this mystery only through faith![22]

Knowing that we are all too human, we can find the example of the Holy Family intimidating. Not only was Jesus a perfect child but his mother had been preserved from the inheritance of original sin, which must have taken her parenting skills to a whole new level. Even St Joseph's example seems impossible to follow since, "by the bond of marriage, there can be no doubt but that Joseph approached as no other person ever could that eminent dignity whereby the Mother

21 Second Vatican Council, *Lumen Gentium* (Dogmatic Constitution on the Church, 1964), 58.
22 St John Paul II, *Redemptoris Mater* ("Mother of the Redeemer"), 17.

of God towers above all creatures".[23] How on earth could we learn from such a family? The answer is that Mary and Joseph also had to advance in their pilgrimage of faith. They too had to listen to, and learn from, their son: "[I]n a sense, Mary as Mother became the first 'disciple' of her Son, the first to whom he seemed to say: 'Follow me,' even before he addressed this call to the Apostles or to anyone else," as St John Paul II explained.[24]

Beyond theories and arguments

St Aelred gives us a convincing reading of the human element of the Gospel story but it is quite clear that his purpose in writing is not simply historical reconstruction. After briefly discussing the verse in which we are told that Jesus grew in wisdom, he tells us that he is going to leave any further discussion to those "who revel in arguing about such things".[25] He knows that his readers don't want "theories and arguments" but instead want his words to bring them "the beginning of devotion to raise your mind to God".[26] St Aelred's work is a great example of *lectio divina* in action and the value of *lectio divina* is that it prevents us from treating the Bible like a dead object in need of dissection, but reminds us that it is one of the means by which the living Word still speaks to his people. That is why St Aelred explains that his approach will be to "leave out the unimportant historical details, and try to come to some really deep understanding of the spiritual meaning of this event in our Lord's life, asking Him to give us grace and guidance in what we say".[27]

---

23 Leo XIII, *Quamquam pluries* ("On Devotion to St Joseph"), 3.
24 St John Paul II, *Redemptoris Mater*, 20.
25 St Aelred, *On Jesus at Twelve Years Old*, 34.
26 St Aelred, *On Jesus at Twelve Years Old*, 35.
27 St Aelred, *On Jesus at Twelve Years Old*, 35.

That being the case, we can look afresh at the question of why it took Mary and Joseph three days to find Jesus. The number three is extremely significant in the Bible. Abraham was visited by three men in a mysterious prefiguration of the Trinity. Jonah spent three days in the fish in anticipation of the three days Jesus spent in the tomb. St Paul reminded us of the importance of the three theological virtues: faith, hope and love. So when Luke tells us that Jesus' parents found him after three days, our ears should prick up. There is clearly more to the length of time it took Mary and Joseph to find Jesus than a mere historical description. But what is the significance? To answer that question we need to step away from the finding in the Temple and move to the end of Jesus' life.

In *The Creed in Slow Motion*, Ronald Knox points out that "if it was an astonishing thing that our Lord should die, equally it was an astonishing thing that he should *stay dead*".[28] We take it for granted that he stayed dead for three days but it is certainly not an event that could possibly have been anticipated, which is why Knox writes that every "second during which he stayed dead, on Good Friday and Holy Saturday and Easter Sunday morning was a kind of miracle; a much more remarkable miracle really than his Resurrection".[29] He gives various reasons why Jesus was buried for three days, but his final explanation is that "Our Lord wanted [the disciples] to learn to wait; waiting is good for all of us".[30] Those three days matter. They were part of God's plan. God knows that we need time to take in his lessons, which takes us back to Jesus at the age of twelve and takes us back to St Aelred's commentary on Luke's account as well. St Aelred points out that in the Temple Jesus "began

28 Ronald Knox, *The Creed in Slow Motion* (Notre Dame, Indiana: Ave Maria Press, 2009), 100.
29 Knox, *The Creed in Slow Motion*, 101.
30 Knox, *The Creed in Slow Motion*, 103.

to unfold the secrets of heaven to those who were learned in the scriptures, for therein lies the priceless treasure of the promise of God's mercy. But he did not open that treasure house to them all at once, but gradually".[31] We might want our children to become saints immediately but it doesn't work like that. There is a process to be gone through. There are temptations and trials to be faced, and temptations and trials to be overcome. We know full well that our children have to grow up physically, but we sometimes forget that spiritual maturity takes time to develop too. And because it takes us time to get where God wants us to be, he adapts his teaching to suit our needs: "At first He listened to them and asked them questions, and then He addressed them openly," St Aelred tells us. He teaches us *gradually*.

In an age of instant gratification, we might struggle with this gradual unfolding of God's will, but there is also a great deal of comfort to be drawn from it. One of the trickiest aspects of being a parent is that we simply don't know how things will turn out. In our workplaces, we often have a sense that a particular approach will yield dividends because it is tried and tested. Either we or our colleagues have done it before to good effect. But when it comes to raising children, there are no set formulae. What works – or seems to work – for other parents may not work for us, either because we are the people we are or because our children are the children they are. To a certain extent, we need to figure it out for ourselves. Even more of a challenge is that we have to keep on figuring it out for ourselves. What works when a child is five may well not work when he or she is ten. What works for one child may not work for a sibling. The unknown future is a real challenge for parents, but we can take comfort from the fact that Jesus taught gradually, that God revealed his plan over many centuries, that Rome was not built in a day.

31 St Aelred, *On Jesus at Twelve Years Old*, 30.

Faith, hope and love

To put it simply, Mary and Joseph's search for Jesus reminds us that we have to be patient. Or, to put it another way, we need to strive for faith and hope, as well as love. We don't know how the future will turn out, we don't know how our children will turn out and we don't know what God wants from each one of us, but we can always remember that God is in charge. We can have faith in him, we can have hope in him and we can love our children with a fierce parental love because we know that God first loved us. As Andy Reed said in his lecture, our job as parents is not to reach perfection but to achieve growth. Bringing up children is not something we accomplish, like getting into our first choice of college or gaining a promotion. It is a process, and a slow process at that.

Raising children is a slow process but we can hold on to the fact that the longer the wait, the greater the joy. Approaching the story of Jesus at twelve years old from a modern perspective, it is easy to dwell on the anxiety his parents seem to have felt. It must have been agonising not to know where Jesus was or whether he was safe. However, looking at St Aelred's book reminds us that another interpretation is possible because he focuses not on anxiety but on joy:

> When I hear [Mary's] question I cannot help asking thee again, why wast thou so sad, my Lady? For it is my opinion that thou wast not filled with any sort of fear for the boy whom thou didst know to be God. Thou wast not afraid that He would suffer from hunger or thirst. No, thy search was not so much motivated by fear, as by the yearning to taste the unspeakable

> delights of His presence which thou hadst lost for even such a little time as three days.[32]

Being absent from her son for three days heightened Our Lady's sense of yearning. Finding him again was a moment of intense joy. And so it is for us today. In this our exile we may well experience a deep yearning for God, but we do so knowing that the future has already arrived. We have already been redeemed and the world's destiny is secure. That is why – as we bring up our children, as we read the story of Jesus aged twelve and as we pray the fifth joyful mystery of the most holy rosary – we too can revel in that same sense of joy that Mary and Joseph knew. If we rely on our own parenting skills, we will never do a good enough job, but if we turn to Christ, we will find a source of inexhaustible joy that can transform our families' lives.

32 St Aelred, *On Jesus at Twelve Years Old*, 31.

He also said, "The kingdom of God is as if someone would scatter seed on the ground, and would sleep and rise night and day, and the seed would sprout and grow, he does not know how. The earth produces of itself, first the stalk, then the head, then the full grain in the head. But when the grain is ripe, at once he goes in with his sickle, because the harvest has come." Mark 4:26-29

"What is the kingdom of God like? And to what should I compare it? It is like a mustard seed that someone took and sowed in the garden; it grew and became a tree, and the birds of the air made nests in its branches." Luke 13:18-19

"Is not this the carpenter's son?" Matthew 13:55

Are parents gardeners or carpenters?

A few years ago, Alison Gopnik, a professor of psychology and philosophy from California, wrote a book called *The Gardener and the Carpenter*, in which she argued that over "the past thirty years, the concept of parenting and the huge industry surrounding it have transformed childcare into obsessive, controlling, and goal-orientated labour".[33] Until recently, parents were content to be parents, but now, she claimed, being a parent has become "a kind of work aimed at creating a successful adult".[34] For Gopnik, this move towards a new kind of work – the work of parenting – is neither grounded in scientific evidence nor good for children. What children really need is to be children, while parents need to be... well, she suggests that parents need to be gardeners.

"Caring for children", she writes, "is like tending a garden, and being a parent is like being a gardener." An alternative approach, she suggests, is to seize control and parent like a carpenter. These two similes set out two fundamentally different ways of seeing the role of the parent. "When we garden... we create a protected and nurturing space for plants to flourish. It takes hard labor and the sweat of our brows, with a lot of exhausted digging and wallowing in manure. And as any gardener knows, our specific plans are always thwarted."[35] Carpenters, by contrast, shape raw material "into a final product that will fit the scheme you had in mind to begin with. And you can assess how good a job you've done by looking at the finished product... Messiness and variability are a carpenter's enemies".[36] There is no doubt which metaphor Alison Gopnik prefers.

---

33 Alison Gopnik, *The Gardener and the Carpenter: what the new science of child development tells us about the relationship between parents and children* (London: Penguin, 2017).

34 Gopnik, *Gardener and Carpenter*, 5.

35 Gopnik, *Gardener and Carpenter*, 18.

36 Gopnik, *Gardener and Carpenter*, 18.

Parents as gardeners

There is a great deal to be said for Gopnik's argument. We live in a world that is target-driven, where outcomes have to be measured to be meaningful and where investment is supposed to provide rewards. We accept an industrial model of education as a self-evident truth: we believe that, if our schools and colleges provide the right input, our children will emerge at the end of the process with the right output, whether that be GCSE grades, A Level passes or a degree. We may not say it out loud but we may also accept the notion that if we bring up our children properly – if we provide them with the right environment, find them the right friends and pass on the correct values – they will turn out all right in the end. And if they don't it's probably our fault. Given the prevalence of that industrial view of the world, it is worth reminding ourselves every now and again of Gopnik's argument that the "most important rewards of being a parent aren't your children's grades and trophies – or even their graduations and weddings. They come from the moment-by-moment physical and psychological joy of being with this particular child, and in that child's moment-by-moment joy in being with you".[37]

Children are often instrumentalised in our contemporary culture. They can easily become a means to an end, whether that be a parent's sense of self-fulfilment or a school's league-table position. In the face of this instrumentalisation we need to be reminded again and again that children are a gift. In the marriage liturgy, we pray that God may gladden the married couple "with your gift of the children they desire". Children are not a right, nor are they a product to be chosen: they are a mysterious gift from God. But they are gifts with lives and minds of their own. That is why we need to nurture and protect them. That is why we need to put in

37 Gopnik, *Gardener and Carpenter*, 10.

hours of hard graft to prepare the ground they need to grow in. However, in the end, despite all our hard work, we have to accept that their futures are not wholly under our control.

Parents as carpenters

The difficulty we face is that the future is so uncertain and we have no second chances, which means that we leave nothing to chance. We attempt to finesse our children into shape or, failing that, we plane down or hack off unsightly edges. We know exactly what we want and so we create a plan that we are determined to follow. We want our children to master the basics and so we supply them with extra maths lessons and ply them with English exercises. We have a sense that certain extra-curricular activities are intrinsically good for them and so organise music lessons and sporting activities. Peer pressure is a problem we are acutely aware of and so we take steps to ensure that our children have the right friends. We set up play dates. We befriend the right parents. We choose our schools carefully, taking whatever steps are necessary to get into the right catchment area.

Parenting like carpenters is problematic but, before we ditch the simile altogether, we need to be aware of the fact that there are also problems with the dichotomy between gardeners and carpenters that Alison Gopnik sets up, problems that quickly become apparent when we look at the Bible. The first and most inconvenient fact is that Jesus Christ was himself a carpenter. As the great French writer and philosopher Fabrice Hadjadj reminds us, God didn't simply become man: he became a carpenter. He could have become a shepherd or a vine dresser, a priest or a lawyer, but instead he became a carpenter.[38] This seems a strange choice of profession if carpentry means hacking recalcitrant pieces of wood into shape but, of course, that is

38 Fabrice Hadjadj, *Résurrection mode d'emploi* (Paris: Magnificat, 2016), 135.

not what carpentry is and that is not what Jesus did. As Pope Benedict once taught, "in the New Testament, the word 'tecton' appears, which was the profession of the Lord Jesus before his public ministry. We usually translate the word as 'carpenter', because at that time houses were made mainly of wood. But more than a 'carpenter', he was an 'artisan' who must have been able to do all that was required in building a house".[39] Jesus was an artisan, a skilled worker, who learned his craft from his father. There was nothing crude about the work he did. In the same talk, Pope Benedict XVI went on to explain the significance of God's chosen profession:

> In the Greek world, intellectual work alone was considered worthy of a free man. Manual work was left to slaves. The biblical religion is quite different. Here, the Creator – who according to a beautiful image, made man with his own hands – appears exactly as the example of a man who works with his hands, and in so doing works with his brain and his heart. Man imitates the Creator so that this world given to him by the Creator may be an inhabitable world. This is apparent in the biblical narrative from the very start. But in the end, the nobility and grandeur of this work strongly emerges from the fact that Jesus was a "tecton", an "artisan", a "worker".[40]

39 Benedict XVI, "Address of His Holiness Benedict XVI to the Employees who Worked to Renovate his Private Apartments", Vatican Website (23 December 2006), <https://w2.vatican.va/content/benedict-xvi/en/speeches/2005/december/documents/hf_ben_xvi_spe_20051223_appartamento-pontificio.html>, accessed 28 Dec. 2018.

40 Benedict XVI, "Address to Employees".

What does all this mean for us as parents? It means, on one level, that we need to take the notion of craftsmanship seriously. In reaction against the blandness of consumer culture, we are beginning to yearn again for anything that bears the mark of human ingenuity rather than the stamp of the machine.[41] We have come to appreciate, with St John Paul II, that work "is a good thing for man – a good thing for his humanity – because through work man not only transforms nature, adapting it to his own needs, but he also achieves fulfilment as a human being and indeed in a sense becomes 'more a human being'".[42] Craftsmanship is good not simply because the craftsman produces beautiful products but because the act of making beautiful objects makes the craftsman more human. His work becomes part of God's plan. The same is true of parents' work. Children are a good in themselves – a far greater good than even the most beautiful work of craftsmanship – but parents' work is also good for parents themselves. We become better people when we engage in our God-given task of bringing up our children.

The work of parents

Alison Gopnik is quite right to be critical of the idea that parenting is a form of work that is goal-directed, but that doesn't mean that we should throw the notion of work out completely. In our contemporary world, work is not taken seriously unless it results in certain well-defined – and lucrative – outcomes. As a consequence, the work of parents, and especially the work of mothers, is often undervalued simply because it is not paid. However, if work has an inherent, God-given dignity – if, in fact, we become

41 See the work of Matthew Crawford and Richard Sennett, in particular.
42 St John Paul II, *Laborem Exercens* ("Through Work"), 9.

more human through our work – then the work of parents will always be hugely important for children, for society and for parents themselves.

If work, as St John Paul II taught, brings us fulfilment and makes us more human, then we are ennobled through what we do as parents. Of course, we might struggle to remember this important truth when our baby has kept us awake all night, when our toddler is kicking off about some minor incident, or when our teenager is resolutely refusing to listen to a word we say. The parents' work, on those occasions, seems neither noble nor fulfilling. Nonetheless, the fact remains that "parenting" is good for us, as long as we focus on our children rather than on ourselves. By definition, the parents' work must be entirely "outward-facing": what matters is what we do for our children rather than what we get out of being parents to our children, though, by a divine paradox, wanting the best for our children also brings us great rewards of joy, fulfilment and love.

So let's examine the work of the carpenter in a little more detail and see how the work that Jesus did for most of his life can help us with the daily challenge of raising our children. The first point to make is that Jesus wasn't simply a carpenter: he was also a "carpenter's son". He learned his craft from his father. Sadly, I am not well known for my carpentry skills. Curtain rails have a tendency to fall off the wall when I have put them up. And I still suffer acute embarrassment when reminded of the moment I proudly told a friend I had put up a shelf only to see it collapse when he put his cup of tea on it. Nonetheless, I do look back with pleasure on a particular occasion when my dad and I worked on a carpentry project together.

As my wife and I were waiting to adopt our first daughter, I decided it would be a good idea to make her a wooden dog on wheels. I had a very clear idea of what I wanted – the tail had to wag for a start – and so I put the project to my dad, not least because he was more technically competent than I. He took up the idea enthusiastically and so we worked happily together in his garage, cutting the outline of the body with a fretsaw, trimming the base to size and fitting the wheels. We had difficulties with the ears and tail until my mum kindly stepped up to the mark with some leather offcuts and created a pair of superbly floppy ears and an impressively wagging tail. Some of my original ideas were adapted as we went along and I had to accept that some of my plans weren't workable at all, but gradually the toy started to emerge. Before too long the dog was completed and we all felt pretty happy with the final product. It may not have been craftsmanship that William Morris would have been proud of, but we felt a real sense of achievement and were delighted when my daughter arrived and started wheeling it around the house.

Attention and adaptability in an age of distraction

The creation of any object requires attention. We need to pay attention to the work in hand and we need to be attentive to the people we are working with, especially if they are also the people we are learning from. The difficulty we face in our digital world is that we find it difficult to be attentive to anything or anyone. We find it harder than ever to stay on task, to concentrate for even short stretches of time, and to finish what we have started. One of the great benefits of manual labour is that it takes us into what Matthew Crawford has called the world beyond our head: when cutting the outline of a dog's body with a fretsaw, we had to exist in the world beyond our heads if only to ensure that we didn't do ourselves an injury.[43] And it's not so different with children.

43 Matthew Crawford, *The World Beyond Your Head: how to flourish in an age of distraction* (London: Penguin, 2015).

They also draw us out of ourselves. The crucial question is how we respond to them when they draw us out of ourselves in that way. Are we attentive in the way that carpenters are attentive to their work, or do we react in the moment before withdrawing back into our own separate life? The constant temptation is to live alone together, as the American author Sherry Turkle puts it in an evocative phrase.[44] In the world we inhabit today, the temptation is to live essentially separate lives, even when we share a house. However, parents are called to live fully with their children. By playing games together, reading books together or going on walks together, we show appreciation for them as people and also show them how to pay attention to the world beyond their heads. And if some of those activities seem unrealistic with older children, we can at least spend time in the same room as them even if we are each doing different activities.

I am not suggesting that paying attention to the world with our children is a miracle cure for the sickness of our modern age, but I agree with Matthew Crawford that "the question of what to attend to is a question of what to value",[45] which is perhaps another way of saying that "where your treasure is, there your heart will be also" (Matthew 6:21). I also acknowledge that the selective attention we give to our children can often be a survival mechanism, a way of coping with constant demands and a lack of time and energy. Being a parent can be a fraught business and there are no easy solutions to that problem either, though being adaptable is always a good place to start.

The carpentry project I worked on with my dad was certainly goal-orientated but that didn't mean that we stuck rigidly to our blueprint. The nature of the material with which we worked

44 Sherry Turkle, *Alone Together: why we expect more from technology and less from each other* (New York: Basic Books, 2017).

45 Crawford, *World Beyond Your Head*, 5.

necessitated changes, as did our technical prowess (or lack of it, in my case). We adapted as we went along, finding that some changes worked out better than expected and that sometimes compromises were required. Just like carpenters, we have to be adaptable as parents. Each child is unique. What works for one child will not necessarily work for another. Parental plans are scuppered by unexpected illnesses, unexpected changes of mood or unexpected opportunities. The weather is changeable. Children are changeable. And we are changeable too. All of which means that sticking to our guns is not always a sensible parenting strategy. Consistency is good: a stubborn refusal to adapt is not. However, when we are both attentive and adaptable we have the essential tools that any carpenter and any parent needs.

Gardening reconsidered

So, if parents really are like carpenters in their attentiveness and adaptability, does that mean we have to reject the gardening metaphor altogether? Not at all, if only because, as Avi I. Mintz has argued, it is entirely possible to use the gardening metaphor to support parenting models that are diametrically opposed to the ones Alison Gopnik promotes in *The Gardener and the Carpenter*.[46] For Gopnik, carpentry is all about shaping your material "into a final product that will fit the scheme you had in mind to begin with", whereas gardening is about creating "a protected and nurturing space for plants to flourish".[47] Carpentry is goal-orientated; gardening is about letting go. We have already seen how that description doesn't do justice to carpentry and it is certainly possible to argue that it doesn't accurately describe gardening either. Gardening, for me, is very clearly

46 Avi I. Mintz, "The present, past, and future of the gardening metaphor in education", *Oxford Review of Education*, 44 (4) (2018), 414-424.
47 Gopnik, *Gardener and Carpenter*, 18.

goal-orientated. I want my tomato plants to produce lots of tomatoes. I want the slugs to stay away from my cabbages. When I plant bulbs, I want them to flower.

What is more, just as carpentry can never be regarded as simply one profession among others (because God became a carpenter), neither can the garden's central place in the scriptures be ignored. There is no getting away from the fact that "the Lord God planted a garden in Eden, in the east; and there he put the man whom he had formed" (Genesis 2:8). It is not an inconsequential detail that Adam and Eve "heard the sound of the Lord God walking in the garden at the time of the evening breeze, and the man and his wife hid themselves from the presence of the Lord God among the trees of the garden" (Genesis 3:8). And that's just the start. As the references to gardens pile up, we need to consider why they feature so prominently in the Bible.

The answer to that question begins in the book of Genesis and ends either in the Garden of Gethsemane (where the "'Yes' of Christ reverses the 'No' of our first parents in the Garden of Eden"[48]) or at Calvary (where "there was a garden in the place where he was crucified, and in the garden there was a new tomb in which no one had ever been laid"(John 19:41). Sin and death entered the world because Adam and Eve ate from the tree of the knowledge of good and evil, but sin and death were conquered through Christ's death on the tree of Calvary. What began in a garden ends in a garden through Christ's great act of recapitulation, to use a term from St Irenaeus that we will return to in a later chapter.

Gardens are important in scripture but so too is the gardener, as we see in the well-known conversation between Mary Magdalene and Jesus after his resurrection:

---

48 St John Paul II, *Rosarium Virginis Mariae* ("The Rosary of the Virgin Mary"), 22.

> Jesus said to her, "Woman, why are you weeping? For whom are you looking?" Supposing him to be the gardener, she said to him, "Sir, if you have carried him away, tell me where you have laid him, and I will take him away." Jesus said to her, "Mary!" She turned and said to him in Hebrew, "Rabbouni!" (which means Teacher). **John 20:15-16**

The usual interpretation of this passage is that Mary failed to recognise Jesus because she was blinded by grief. She thought he was the gardener but then corrected herself and called him "teacher". However, another way of interpreting the same passage is to suggest that maybe she was right on both counts: Jesus was both a gardener and a teacher. The same Lord who walked "in the garden [of Eden] in the cool of the day" was now walking in the garden outside Jerusalem. The same Lord who made the Garden of Eden was now remaking the world (and its gardens) through his perfect sacrifice on the cross. The gardener was at work.

Parables and gardens

It is striking how often Jesus turned to the natural world for his parables. We might have expected him to draw more often on his own profession of carpentry, but he much more commonly drew on the natural world with which all his hearers would have been familiar. Take the parable of the growing seed and the parable of the mustard seed as examples:

"The kingdom of God is as if someone would scatter seed on the ground, and would sleep and rise night and day, and the seed would sprout and grow, he does not know how. The earth produces of itself, first the stalk, then the head, then the full grain in the head. But when the grain is ripe, at once he goes in with his sickle, because the harvest has come."
Mark 4:26-29

"What is the kingdom of God like? And to what should I compare it? It is like a mustard seed that someone took and sowed in the garden; it grew and became a tree, and the birds of the air made nests in its branches."
Luke 13:18-19

We sometimes think of parables as simple allegories with only one meaning, but the truth is much more complex and interesting than that. As Pope Benedict XVI explained in the first volume of his books on *Jesus of Nazareth*, parables are fundamentally "hidden and multi-layered invitations to faith in Jesus as the 'Kingdom of God in person'".[49] In Pope Benedict's interpretation, the "time of Jesus, the time of the disciples, is the time of sowing and of the seed. The 'Kingdom of God' is present in seed form. ... The seed is the presence of what is to come in the future. In the seed, that which is to come is already here in a hidden way. It is the presence of a promise".[50] But the parable is even richer

49 Joseph Ratzinger, *Jesus of Nazareth: from the baptism in the Jordan to the transfiguration* (London: Bloomsbury, 2007), 188.
50 Ratzinger, *Jesus of Nazareth*, 190.

than that because "Jesus is not only the sower who scatters the seed of God's word, but also the seed that falls into the earth in order to die and so to bear fruit".[51] The parable of the mustard seed, then, is not simply a story about the importance of faith (though it is also that): it has a wider application. Its primary purpose is to speak to us about Christ himself.

Such is the richness of the parables that they can yield many meanings. So what do these parables teach us about parenting? Surely the message that comes through Jesus' description of the way that the seed sprouts and grows while the man sleeps and rises "night and day" is that time matters. Just as seeds need time, so too do we and so too do our children. It is worth being reminded in our age of instant gratification that God's speed is not our speed. His time is quite different from ours. Ronald Knox has a wonderful passage about this in *The Creed in Slow Motion*, where he writes:

> Our Lord... wanted the whole of his merciful design for our redemption to unroll itself gradually before our eyes, like a kind of slow-motion picture; never hurrying, never giving us the opportunity of saying, "Stop a minute, I haven't quite taken that in yet." He wouldn't just come to earth, he would spend thirty-three years on earth. He wouldn't just appear suddenly and scatter miracles over the countryside in the course of an afternoon; he would spend three years going about and doing good. He wouldn't just die for us; he would hang there, three whole hours, on the Cross, so that we could watch him and take

51 Ratzinger, *Jesus of Nazareth*, 191.

> it all in. And he wouldn't just die and rise again; he would spend part of three days in the tomb... Nothing impresses us so much, when we read the account of God's dealings with his creation, either in science or in history, as the majestic slowness of his movements. And God made Man did not lose the characteristics of Godhead; he went to work very slowly, for all the world to see that he was God.[52]

Parables and time

Maybe this is the most important way in which parents are like gardeners. We need to take our time and accept that God will be taking his time too. We live in a world that demands instant results, but children are not products to be churned out at an industrial pace. The seed grows; we know not how, but still it grows. Our children are shaped and changed by the slow processes of love, though we may not know how or always see the evidence. As gardeners – as parents – we need the virtue of patience, we need to learn to accept that our job is to plant the seeds and that God's job is to see that they grow. Of course, this is easier said than done. It is easy to give way to despair when our children look as if they might be going off the rails (to use an image that is very much not drawn from nature), but that is where the primary meaning of the parable comes in. We need not just patience but faith as well.

We know that children need love over time but we also know that we have only one chance. If we get it wrong we can't go back and reparent our children. That is why we leave nothing to chance, why we organise extra tuition or fill

52 Ronald Knox, *The Creed in Slow Motion* (Notre Dame, Indiana: Ave Maria Press, 2009), 103-104.

every moment of our children's time with activities. We know – or think we know – that if we don't step in, our children will succumb to the weaknesses that all children are prone to. But the parable of the sower reminds us that we need to trust in God *over time*. If we dig up the seed to see how it is growing, we won't speed up the process: we will stop it from happening at all.

That is why, as parent–gardeners, we need to develop a decent theology of compost. I have two compost bins in my garden, one of which is beginning to yield a rich crop of good-quality fertiliser, while the other seems to be doing very little at all. When I started composting, I threw anything and everything into the compost bin. Garden waste was an obvious choice and so too was old hay from the rabbits' hutch. In they went, I closed the lid and I assumed that a dark rich humus would appear several months later. It didn't.

The reason my first compost bin failed to yield dividends was that I hadn't appreciated that there is more to composting than simply dumping unwanted waste. What a good compost heap needs is warmth, water, air, a good mix of green and brown compostable material and plenty of time. In a similar way, what our children need is warmth, water, air, the ups and downs of life, lots of prayer and plenty of time. What goes into the compost bin of our lives is the same messy material that God can turn to his good purposes. Sometimes, that distinctly unpromising material simply sits and festers. At other times, it breaks down into rich fertilising material. What makes the difference is not the material that makes up our lives – that never bears too close an examination – but what we do with it. If we don't give our children the material they need – time and the nutrient-rich experiences that go into any holy, healthy childhood – they won't develop good compost. Without love, prayer and the sacraments, the messiness of their lives won't be transformed into rich and life-sustaining soil.

Gardeners and carpenters

So, are parents gardeners or carpenters? The best answer is that we are both. Like carpenters and gardeners, we need to be attentive and adaptable. Like gardeners and carpenters, we need to be patient. Like both gardeners and carpenters, we can be goal-orientated as long as we don't become rigid (and as long as we remember that our main goal for our children should be that they become saints[53]). There is nothing inherently wrong with either simile, but we will certainly get the most out of the imagery, and out of our own daily efforts, if we nourish our view of these two noble professions by drawing from the rich well of the scriptures. What Jesus taught two thousand years ago can still help us as parents today.

53 Benedict XVI, "Address of the Holy Father to Pupils", Vatican Website (17 September 2010), <https://w2.vatican.va/content/benedict-xvi/en/speeches/2010/september/documents/hf_ben-xvi_spe_20100917_mondo-educ.html#ADDRESS_OF_THE_HOLY_FATHER_TO_PUPILS.>, accessed 23 Oct. 2017.

II

Children

After three days they found him in the temple, sitting among the teachers, listening to them and asking them questions. And all who heard him were amazed at his understanding and his answers. When his parents saw him they were astonished; and his mother said to him, "Child, why have you treated us like this? Look, your father and I have been searching for you in great anxiety." He said to them, "Why were you searching for me? Did you not know that I must be in my Father's house?" But they did not understand what he said to them. Then he went down with them and came to Nazareth, and was obedient to them. His mother treasured all these things in her heart. And Jesus increased in wisdom and in years, and in divine and human favour. Luke 2:46-52

What can we learn from the twelve-year-old Jesus?

In *Last Child in the Woods*, Richard Louv reminisces about his childhood in the 1950s, telling us that "I knew my woods and my fields; I knew every bend in the creek and dip in the beaten dirt paths. I wandered those woods even in my dreams. A kid today can likely tell you about the Amazon rain forest – but not about the last time he or she explored the woods in solitude, or lay in a field listening to the wind and watching the clouds move".[1] What we see in Louv's description is the latest stage in our changing relationship with the land. In the murky afterglow of the Industrial Revolution we began to romanticise the countryside, but, more recently, we have given up on it altogether, preferring electronic gadgetry to the slow changes of the seasons and the natural challenges that being in the world presents.

Louv is concerned about our current situation, contrasting it with an earlier age when our forefathers lived in a far closer relationship with nature, so we might wonder what it was like to grow up two thousand years ago. As Mary and Joseph headed home to Nazareth, was Jesus exploring the woods in solitude, or lying in a field listening to the wind and watching the clouds move? We know that he had an appreciation of the beauty of nature, since he spoke to his disciples about the birds of the air and the lilies of the field, but did he wander free, as Richard Louv remembers doing in the 1950s, because his parents had never heard of tiger mums or helicopter parenting?

A closer look at the New Testament suggests that we have to be very cautious about reading our current concerns back into the biblical narrative. Mary and Joseph were not permissive parents and the lesson that the twelve-year-

1 Richard Louv, *Last Child in the Woods: saving our children from nature-deficit disorder* (London: Atlantic Books, 2010), 1-2.

old Jesus has to teach us is not to back off and just let our children be. Jesus may have asked his disciples why they worried about clothing, telling them instead to "consider the lilies of the field" (Matthew 6:28), but he certainly didn't romanticise the lilies. In fact, he was utterly matter-of-fact about their fate, commenting that "today" they may be alive but "tomorrow" they will be "thrown into the oven" (Matthew 6:30). There is not much of a sense here that he was nostalgic about lying in a field while listening to the wind and watching the clouds move.

The Gospel writers do not suggest that Jesus was used to a life of carefree independence, unfettered by the demands of anxiety-ridden parents. Indeed, a closer look at the story of Jesus at the age of twelve suggests that there were clear limits to the independence he was given because, after travelling for a day, Mary and Joseph "started to look for him *among their relatives* and friends" (Luke 2:44 – my emphasis). Jesus was not wandering free for a day while his parents took a well-earned break. He was travelling, as far as they knew, with members of the family.

In the West, conceptions of the family have narrowed considerably over the years. We now tend to think of the nuclear family as *the* family, but clearly that wasn't the case in Jesus' day. The first decision Mary took after the annunciation was to go "with haste to a Judean town in the hill country, where she entered the house of Zechariah and greeted Elizabeth" (Luke 1:39-40). Not only that but she "remained with her for about three months" (Luke 1:56). There are further hints of the closeness of family bonds in the next few lines of Luke's Gospel too, since it was "her neighbours and relatives" who rejoiced with Elizabeth when she gave birth (Luke 1:58). Whatever lesson the twelve-year-old Jesus has to teach us, it is not that children should be given total independence.

And yet it is a prevailing myth of our age that it is good for young people to leave home as soon as it is financially viable for them to do so. We are told that they need to go away to college or university to learn to become truly independent. It is almost a matter of faith that they must move away, establish themselves and live lives of their own as soon as is humanly possible. This idea may be embedded in our culture, but it comes with a downside. A colleague once told me that her father encouraged her and her siblings to move away from home and live independent lives as soon as they became adults, not through any selfish motivation but because he genuinely believed that would be the best course for them. The children duly did so, fanning out across the country and becoming successful in their own fields. But when their father became seriously ill and needed his children, it was incredibly difficult for them to be with him for any extended length of time, as they all had jobs to hold down and families of their own to care for. They did their best, but it was clearly a very difficult time for them all. Contrast this situation with the one we find in the Gospels, where Jesus began his public ministry at the age of thirty and, even then, clearly remained close to his mother.

Listening and answering

So what does the story of Jesus in the Temple have to teach us today? For St Aelred the answer was clear. Through his actions, Jesus provided us with a "model of humility" and showed the young "how they should be silent before those who are old and wise. If they will listen and ask questions, they can learn great things".[2] Later in his book he went even further, explaining that, "as Jesus Christ, true God and true man, sits there, He is an example to us all. As He listens, He shows young children how they must be attentive to God's

2 St Aelred, *On Jesus at Twelve Years Old*, 30.

word. His questions show young people how they must inquire diligently into the truths of their faith. He shows those who are older how they must spread God's message to men, just as He, although only twelve years old at the time, gave instruction to the elders and doctors in Jerusalem".[3]

St Aelred is surely right to draw our attention to Jesus' actions. Though he is the Son of God, he begins by "listening" to the teachers in the Temple and "asking them questions". What a wonderful example of divine humility in action! What Luke doesn't explicitly spell out is that the same teachers must have asked him questions too, because "all who heard him were amazed at his understanding and *his answers*" (Luke 2:47 – my emphasis). The order is important. Listening comes first and answers come after. If this was Jesus' approach, it makes a lot of sense for us to adopt it as ours too and yet, if we are honest, when it comes to our relationships with God and with our children, we often answer first and listen after.

This might seem like a very simple lesson but it is one that the first disciples struggled to take on board. Even the disciples closest to Jesus needed to hear God's voice from the cloud at the transfiguration telling them, "This is my Son, the Beloved; with him I am well pleased; listen to him!" (Matthew 17:5). We get much the same message from the story of Martha and Mary. In the busyness of our family lives, we can all identify with Martha's failure simply to sit at the feet of Jesus and listen to him, but Jesus' message to her was uncompromising:

> Now as they went on their way, he entered a certain village, where a woman named Martha welcomed

3 St Aelred, *On Jesus at Twelve Years Old*, 44.

> him into her home. She had a sister named Mary, who sat at the Lord's feet and listened to what he was saying. But Martha was distracted by her many tasks; so she came to him and asked, "Lord, do you not care that my sister has left me to do all the work by myself? Tell her then to help me." But the Lord answered her, "Martha, Martha, you are worried and distracted by many things; there is need of only one thing. Mary has chosen the better part, which will not be taken away from her." **Luke 10:38-42**

What the twelve-year-old Jesus teaches is that the same lesson applies to us today. We can all find reasons not to listen to God, our spouse and our children, but, like Mary, we all need to choose the good portion. We all need to stop and listen, because it is only when we listen that we draw close to other people.

A joyful mystery

The importance of listening to others is the first lesson that the twelve-year-old Jesus has to teach us, but it is not the only one, especially if we remember that the story of the finding in the Temple does not take place in a vacuum. It is part of a sequence of events, running from the annunciation to the visitation to the birth of Jesus and the presentation in the Temple. It is part of a sequence that we recall when we say the joyful mysteries of the rosary.

That being the case, it is worth stepping aside for a moment to establish exactly what is going on when we recite the rosary. This might seem like a basic question but it takes us right to the heart of what the young Jesus can teach us today. In his great apostolic letter, *Rosarium Virginis*

Mariae ("The Rosary of the Virgin Mary"), St John Paul II wrote these remarkable sentences: "The Rosary mystically transports us to Mary's side as she is busy watching over the human growth of Christ in the home of Nazareth. This enables her to train us and to mould us with the same care, until Christ is 'fully formed' in us (cf. Gal 4:19)."[4]

The idea that we are mystically transported to Mary's side is no idle metaphor: St John Paul II really meant it. In prayer we remain in time but draw close to God who is beyond time. Or rather, in prayer, God, who is beyond time but who has already entered time in the person of his Son, draws us to him.[5] It is the Holy Spirit who "helps us in our weakness; for we do not know how to pray as we ought, but the Spirit himself intercedes with sighs too deep for words", as St Paul teaches in his Letter to the Romans.[6]

When we pray the rosary we are not simply recalling the events of Jesus' life, but are drawn to Mary's side as she experiences those events during her own pilgrimage of faith. "The Christian liturgy not only recalls the events that saved us," the *Catechism* tells us, "but actualises them, makes them present." In the same way, the rosary is not simply a way of remembering the key events of Jesus' life but is one of the means that God uses to make them present for us. Mary is not a distant historical figure whose example should inspire us; rather, she is a living presence in the Church. When we pray the rosary, we are not thinking about her: we are with her. Having been taken up into heaven, she didn't lay aside her work as Mother of the Church but is able to be with us in an even more wonderful way:

---

4 St John Paul II, *Rosarium Virginis Mariae* ("The Rosary of the Virgin Mary"), 15.

5 In *The Spirit of the Liturgy*, Joseph Ratzinger wrote that when Jesus gives himself to be crucified "time is drawn into what reaches beyond time. The real interior act, though it does not exist without the exterior, transcends time, but since it comes from time, time can again and again be brought into it". Joseph Ratzinger, *The Spirit of the Liturgy* (San Francisco: Ignatius Press, 2000), 56.

6 Romans 8:26.

> This motherhood of Mary in the order of grace continues uninterruptedly from the consent which she loyally gave at the Annunciation and which she sustained without wavering beneath the cross, until the eternal fulfilment of all the elect. Taken up to heaven she did not lay aside this saving office but by her manifold intercession continues to bring us the gifts of eternal salvation.[7]

When we pray the rosary, Mary can train us and mould us with the same care she showed for her own son. Her joy becomes our joy. Her pilgrimage of faith makes ours possible too.

The newness of prayer in the fullness of time

Jesus listened to the teachers in the Temple and answered their questions, but he listened to Mary and answered her question too. Both that answer ("Why were you searching for me? Did you not know that I must be in my Father's house?") and the listening ("he went down with [Mary and Joseph] and came to Nazareth, and was obedient to them") are important. And yet we might struggle to see how the two go together. How could Jesus go missing for three days and also be said to be obedient to his parents? A beautifully profound passage from the *Catechism* might help us begin to formulate an answer:

---

7 *Lumen Gentium*, 62.

> The Son of God who became Son of the Virgin also learned to pray according to his human heart. He learns the formulas of prayer from his mother, who kept in her heart and meditated upon all the "great things" done by the Almighty. He learns to pray in the words and rhythms of the prayer of his people, in the synagogue at Nazareth and the Temple at Jerusalem. But his prayer springs from an otherwise secret source, as he intimates at the age of twelve: "I must be in my Father's house." Here the newness of prayer in the fullness of time begins to be revealed: his *filial prayer*, which the Father awaits from his children, is finally going to be lived out by the only Son in his humanity, with and for men.[8]

On a human level, Jesus learns from his parents and from his people, but the source of his prayer is God the Father. That is why the finding in the Temple is such a crucial moment for Mary and for us. It signals the moment that Jesus' fundamental orientation towards his Father in heaven becomes apparent: "He is in the Temple not as a rebel against his parents, but precisely as the obedient one, acting out the same obedience that leads to the Cross and the resurrection."[9] Luke is also absolutely clear that, having spent time in his Father's house, Jesus returns to Nazareth with Mary and Joseph and is obedient to them. He also tells us that "Jesus increased in wisdom and in years, and in divine and human favour" (Luke 2:52). To put it simply, Jesus wasn't obedient because he had been disobedient before,

8 *Catechism of the Catholic Church*, 2599.

9 Joseph Ratzinger, *Jesus of Nazareth: the infancy narratives* (London: Bloomsbury, 2012), 124.

nor did he reject his earthly parents in order to pay exclusive attention to his Father in heaven.

A very modern temptation is to set these two fundamental obligations – to God and to parents – in opposition to each other. We want the best for our children but we might be tempted to think that if we let God in on the act he will frustrate our plans. We might well recall with nervousness the passage in Luke's Gospel when "a woman in the crowd raised her voice and said to him, 'Blessed is the womb that bore you and the breasts that nursed you!'" only for Jesus to reply, "Blessed rather are those who hear the word of God and obey it!" (Luke 11:27-28). Or the time when Jesus was told that "your mother and your brothers are standing outside, wanting to see you" only for him to reply, "My mother and my brothers are those who hear the word of God and do it" (Luke 8:20-21). We need to recall, however, that there is no better example of someone who heard the word of God and did it than Our Lady herself. Jesus was certainly not rejecting his mother with this answer but was explaining how his family – a family that began on earth with the Holy Family – would continue to grow.

What the twelve-year-old Jesus taught his mother in the Temple, in other words, and what he has to teach us today is that if we "strive first for the kingdom of God and his righteousness... all these things will be given to you as well" (Matthew 6:33). If we put God first, we too will see our children increase "in wisdom and in years, and in divine and human favour".

Presentations in the Temple

What we are beginning to see in this chapter is that we have to see the story of the finding in the Temple in its context if we are going to have any chance of learning the lessons that the twelve-year-old Jesus has to teach us today. The story reveals the fullness of its message only when seen both in relation to the story that precedes it in Luke's Gospel – the presentation in the Temple – and also in relation to the story that prefigures it in the Old Testament: the calling of Samuel.

The work of Blessed Columba Marmion can help us understand what Mary and Joseph were doing when they took Jesus to the Temple when he was forty days old. Marmion reminds us that the Jewish law prescribed that firstborn males had to be presented to the Lord and also that "the child could be 'bought back' by an offering, large or otherwise – a lamb or a pair of pigeons – according to the family's financial position".[10] In Mary and Joseph's case, the offering was a pair of pigeons because they were poor. This brief insight into Jesus' background is fascinating but it makes even more sense if we look further back, to the story of Hannah in the Old Testament. In deep distress because she had not conceived, she prayed:

> O Lord of hosts, if only you will look on the misery of your servant, and remember me, and not forget your servant, but will give to your servant a male child, then I will set him before you as a nazirite until the day of his death. He shall drink neither wine nor intoxicants, and no razor shall touch his head. **1 Samuel 1:11**

After the birth of her child, Samuel, she kept her vow and presented him to the Lord, leaving him with Eli the priest rather than buying him back with an offering. She then poured out her soul to God in a song of praise that began:

10 Marmion, *Christ in His Mysteries*, 184.

My heart exults in the Lord;
  my strength is exalted in my God.
My mouth derides my enemies,
  because I rejoice in my victory.
There is no Holy One like the Lord,
  no one besides you;
  there is no Rock like our God. **1 Samuel 2:1-2**

Like Mary, Hannah conceived only after divine intervention and, like her, she poured out her heart in song to God (Mary's Magnificat drawing beautifully on Hannah's prayer). The similarities do not end there. Both women presented their sons to the Lord and both Samuel and Jesus spent time in the place where God dwelt on earth, Samuel serving Eli and even sleeping "where the ark of God was" (1 Samuel 3:3) and Jesus remaining in Jerusalem to be in his "Father's house" (Luke 2:49). "Samuel", we are told in the Old Testament, "continued to grow both in stature and in favour with the Lord and with the people" (1 Samuel 2:26), just as Jesus "increased in wisdom and in years, and in divine and human favour", as Luke writes in his Gospel, the parallels between the two passages being even clearer in other translations.

But there are differences too because the story of Samuel only prefigures the greater story that was to come. When Samuel heard God's voice, he did not understand what he was hearing because he "did not yet know the Lord, and the word of the Lord had not yet been revealed to him" (1 Samuel 3:7). Jesus, by contrast, knew exactly what God wanted of him. Instead, it was his parents who "did not understand what he said to them". It was a great day when Hannah presented Samuel to Eli but, according to Blessed Columba Marmion, when Mary presented Jesus "God received on that day infinitely more glory in this Temple than

He had received up to then from all the sacrifices and all the holocausts of the Old Law", adding that "the only Victim worthy of God had just been offered to Him".[11]

When Jesus asked Mary if she did not know "that I must be in my Father's house" he was, in a sense, reminding her of what she had already done by presenting him to God when he was just forty days old. He was also reminding her that he was in the very place where he belonged: with the Father, in his house.[12] He was reminding her that his true father was God himself.

So, once we have set the story in its context, what should our response be to the twelve-year-old Jesus? In the first place, we can echo Blessed Columba Marmion's words in thanking "the Virgin Mary for having presented her Divine Son for us. Let us render fervent thanksgiving to Jesus for having offered Himself to His Father for our salvation". But we can do so in the certain knowledge that this offering of Christ to the Father has continued throughout the ages. It happened at the presentation and again when Jesus made the pilgrimage with his family, and it happens still today since "at Holy Mass, Christ offers Himself anew", as Blessed Columba Marmion reminds us.[13] What the twelve-year-old Jesus can teach us is what he teaches us each time we go to Mass: that we need to "unite ourselves with Him, like Him, in a disposition of complete submission of our will to His Heavenly Father".[14]

He teaches us to get our priorities right.

---

11 Marmion, *Christ in His Mysteries*, 186.
12 Ratzinger, *Jesus of Nazareth: the infancy narratives*, 124.
13 Marmion, *Christ in His Mysteries*, 188.
14 Marmion, *Christ in His Mysteries*, 188-189.

The true light, which enlightens everyone, was coming into the world. He was in the world, and the world came into being through him; yet the world did not know him. He came to what was his own, and his own people did not accept him. But to all who received him, who believed in his name, he gave power to become children of God, who were born, not of blood or of the will of the flesh or of the will of man, but of God. John 1:9-13

See what love the Father has given us, that we should be called children of God; and that is what we are. 1 John 3:1

But when the fullness of time had come, God sent his Son, born of a woman, born under the law, in order to redeem those who were under the law, so that we might receive adoption as children. And because you are children, God has sent the Spirit of his Son into our hearts, crying, "Abba! Father!" So you are no longer a slave but a child, and if a child then also an heir, through God Galatians 4:4-7

How do we become children of God?

The *Catechism of the Catholic Church* begins with a truly wonderful passage that encapsulates in just a few short sentences the nature of God's plan for his people:

> God, infinitely perfect and blessed in himself, in a plan of sheer goodness freely created man to make him share in his own blessed life. For this reason, at every time and in every place, God draws close to man. He calls man to seek him, to know him, to love him with all his strength. He calls together all men, scattered and divided by sin, into the unity of his family, the Church. To accomplish this, when the fullness of time had come, God sent his Son as Redeemer and Saviour. In his Son and through him, he invites men to become, in the Holy Spirit, his adopted children and thus heirs of his blessed life.[15]

There is enough in this short passage to inspire us for a lifetime, but I want to home in on the last sentence: God invites us to become his adopted children and thus heirs of his blessed life. What does this mean and how does it happen?

Time after time in the New Testament we hear that we are called to be children of God. Right at the start of his Gospel, John tells us that "to all who received [Jesus], who believed in his name, he gave power to become children of God" (John 1:12), before emphasising the point in his First Letter: "See what love the Father has given us, that we should be called

---

15 *Catechism of the Catholic Church*, 1.

children of God; and that is what we are" (1 John 3:1). This is no metaphor. We really are children of God. We are so used to hearing these words that we can take them for granted, and yet this should be the most wonderful of surprises.

In *Christ, the Life of the Soul*, Blessed Columba Marmion explains that the fatherhood of God is an absolutely fundamental dogma for Catholics. God is Father of the Son from all eternity but he also wants to "extend, so to speak, His Paternity".[16] Marmion expresses this desire in a beautiful way by writing: "By nature, God has only one Son. By love, He will have a multitude of them, without number".[17] He also points out that "to exist, God has need only of Himself and His perfections. Finding all bliss in the perfections of His nature and in the ineffable society of His Persons, He has no need of any creature".[18] And yet he still chooses, through love, to make us his children:

> God means not only to give Himself to us as Supreme Beauty, object of contemplation, but to unite Himself to us, so as to make Himself, so far as is possible, but one with us... How does God effect this magnificent design by which He wishes us to have part in this life which exceeds the dimensions of our nature, which surpasses our nature's own rights and energies, which is not called for by any of its demands, but which, without destroying that nature, showers on it a bliss undreamt-of by the human heart? How will God make us have ineffable "fellowship with" His Divine life so

16 Blessed Columba Marmion, *Christ, the Life of the Soul* (Leominster: Gracewing, 2005), 7.
17 Marmion, *Christ, the Life of the Soul*, 7.
18 Marmion, *Christ, the Life of the Soul*, 17-18.

as to make us sharers of the eternal beatitude? By adopting us as His children.[19]

The grace of supernatural adoption

It is through the grace of supernatural adoption that we become children of God, according to Blessed Columba Marmion. And not just according to him. This explanation goes right back to St Paul, who wrote in his Letter to the Galatians that "God sent his Son, born of a woman, born under the law, in order to redeem those who were under the law, so that we might receive adoption as children" (Galatians 4:4-5). We also hear about adoption repeatedly in the liturgy. On the feast of the Baptism of Our Lord, we pray that God's "children by adoption, reborn of water and the Holy Spirit, may always be well pleasing to you" and, during the Easter Vigil, we pray to God who pours out "the grace of adoption throughout the whole world". We also pray that "through sacred adoption" God will increase the children of his promise and ask that he will stir up "a spirit of adoption" in the Church. These are not incidental details but take us right to the heart of what it means to become children of God.

It is, of course, true that "through Baptism we are freed from sin and reborn as sons of God", as the *Catechism* puts it.[20] However, this rebirth is not entirely separate from our adoption because, as the *Catechism* goes on to explain, it is through baptism that we become the adopted children of God: "Baptism not only purifies from all sins, but also makes the neophyte 'a new creature,' an adopted son of God, who has become a 'partaker of the divine nature,' member of

19 Marmion, *Christ, the Life of the Soul*, 19-20.
20 *Catechism of the Catholic Church*, 1213.

Christ and co-heir with him, and a temple of the Holy Spirit."[21] Through the indwelling of the Holy Spirit, we are drawn into the life of Christ and the process of divinisation begins. Through baptism we begin the process of sharing God's very life and becoming like him. That is a quite amazing thought!

The Greek word St Paul uses for adoption literally means "making or rendering someone a son". It would have been a relatively familiar term to at least some of his readers because adoption was quite common in the Roman Empire, with several emperors adopting a son to ensure a successful transition of power. However, the idea also had roots in the Old Testament. The word is not used in the book of Exodus but, as St Stephen told the council shortly before his martyrdom, Moses was clearly adopted by Pharaoh's daughter: "At this time Moses was born, and was beautiful before God. And he was brought up for three months in his father's house; and when he was exposed, Pharaoh's daughter adopted him and brought him up as her own son" (Acts 7:20-22, Revised Standard Version, Catholic Edition). Moses was not the only person in the Old Testament to be adopted: Esther was adopted by Mordecai and, as we have already seen, Samuel was raised by Eli in the Temple. However, adoption certainly received a new emphasis in the New Testament, an emphasis that was picked up in the liturgy and in the works of authors such as Blessed Columba Marmion.

Healing the primal wound

So what are the implications of our becoming children of God through the grace of supernatural adoption? To tease these implications out, we could usefully turn to some of the thorough work that has been done on the parenting of adopted children. Since we have a sacramental religion, it makes sense to look at earthly matters in the expectation that

---

21 *Catechism of the Catholic Church*, 1265.

they will lead us to heavenly matters. The starting point for most work with adopted children is the acknowledgement that they have all suffered what has been called a "primal wound". This term was first coined by Nancy Newton Verrier, who explains it in this way:

> Many doctors and psychologists now understand that bonding [between the mother and child] doesn't begin at birth, but is a continuum of physiological, psychological, and spiritual events which begin in utero and continue throughout the postnatal bonding period. When this natural evolution is interrupted by a postnatal separation from the biological mother, the resultant experience of abandonment and loss is indelibly imprinted upon the unconscious minds of these children, causing that which I call the "primal wound."[22]

Adoption is always a response to loss, trauma and this deep primal wound. As such, it is more than a legal fiction, a rewriting of legal documents to render someone a child of a new family. Adoption is an event that must always become a process. A process of healing that lasts a lifetime. What is true of natural adoption also holds true, at least to an extent, for supernatural adoption.

Just as adopted children have suffered a primal wound, so too have all people suffered a primal wound: the wound of original sin that separated us from the God who created us. The consequences of this wound – of original sin – can

22 Nancy Newton Verrier, *The Primal Wound: understanding the adopted child* (Baltimore, MD: Gateway Press, 1993), 1.

hardly be overstated. Cut off from the life that God originally intended for us, we have all gone astray. We are the lost sheep that Jesus speaks of in the parable; far from God, we have no hope of salvation unless the good shepherd himself comes in search of us. Original sin has affected us all to the very core of our being, but the good news is that God has chosen to win us back "so that we might receive adoption as children" (Galatians 4:5).

In baptism the stain of sin is washed away and we become adopted children of God. However, in exactly the same way that adopted children do not simply cast off their early life experiences and live as though they had never suffered deep trauma, neither is anyone else able to shake off the effects of sin in their life. This is a central theme of St Paul's letters. On the one hand, he declares with great confidence that "if anyone is in Christ, there is a new creation" (2 Corinthians 5:17) but, on the other, he explains the continuing power of sin, writing that "I do not understand my own actions. For I do not do what I want, but I do the very thing I hate" (Romans 7:15). This may well be a familiar feeling for all of us, but it is especially acute in the lives of adopted children, who are not always in control of their own actions. Desperately wanting to behave in one way, they can be drawn back to destructive ways of behaviour because of that early childhood trauma. Life for everyone, adopted or not, is a constant internal battle: "For I delight in the law of God in my inmost self, but I see in my members another law at war with the law of my mind, making me captive to the law of sin that dwells in my members" (Romans 7:22-23). In recent years, it has become increasingly clear how deep-rooted the adopted child's primal wound really is. By contrast, the tendency in contemporary society is to play down – or ignore altogether – the deep-rooted impact of original sin. In a world in which the cruelties we inflict on each other have become clearer with every passing decade, we are curiously reluctant to accept the wisdom of the Church when it comes to identifying the source of those horrors.

All this sounds very bleak but, of course, it is not the end of the story. The very man who wrote about the powerful impact of original sin in our lives was the same man who declared just a few verses later that there is "now no condemnation for those who are in Christ Jesus. For the law of the Spirit of life in Christ Jesus has set you free from the law of sin and death" (Romans 8:1-2). Developing his argument further, St Paul reminded the Christians in Rome that "the Spirit of God dwells in you" (Romans 8:9). And if God really lives in us then we no longer need to be encumbered by sin. We are a new creation. In fact, the presence of the Holy Spirit – God himself – in our hearts is the reason why we are newly alive, truly the adopted children of God:

> When we cry, "Abba! Father!" it is that very Spirit bearing witness with our spirit that we are children of God, and if children, then heirs, heirs of God and joint heirs with Christ – if, in fact, we suffer with him so that we may also be glorified with him. **Romans 8:15-17**

St Paul's letters are gloriously uplifting testaments to the power of God at work in the world, but we may still struggle to work out how we can apply these insights in the lives of our own families. It might, therefore, be worth stepping away from St Paul for a moment to look at the work that has been done in recent years to help the parents of adopted children. Since we are all the adopted children of God, we could do a lot worse than draw on the insights of those who have worked intensively with adopted children.

Parenting with PACE

A particularly insightful author is the clinical psychologist Dan Hughes, who has developed a model for healthy parent–child relationships composed of four key components: playfulness, acceptance, curiosity and empathy. Bringing these components together in one acronym, we can therefore talk about the importance of parenting with PACE. Hughes may not have been writing for a predominantly Christian readership but it is striking how many of his ideas tie in with a Christian understanding of human nature. He points out, for example, that a "central feature of playfulness is the sense of openness to possibility that it generates: Play can generate hope".[23] Hughes' focus is very much on playfulness as a means of building a closer bond between parent and child but, applying his ideas more widely, we might also see in his approach a means of developing the theological virtue of hope in the lives of our families.

The second aspect of PACE is acceptance, which is also explained in a way that fits in perfectly with a Christian understanding of relationships: "When parents are with their infant," Hughes writes, "they tend to be unconditionally in love with him or her, accepting the baby as he or she is, with no strings attached. Parents do not evaluate the rightness or wrongness of the baby's behavior or judge him or her to be 'good' or 'bad'."[24] "Judge not, that you be not judged" might be another way of putting it.

The C in PACE stands for curiosity. Curiosity is a problematic word in some ways, so we need to be very clear about what Hughes means by it. In his definition, curiosity is all about

---

23 Daniel Hughes and Jonathan Baylin, *Brain-Based Parenting: the neuroscience of caregiving for healthy attachment* (New York: W.W. Norton & Company, 2012), 107.

24 Hughes and Baylin, *Brain-Based Parenting*, 111.

parents being "fully immersed in getting to know their infant unconditionally. This is not a rational exercise but rather an act that fully engages parents reflectively, emotionally, spiritually and viscerally. As they get to know their infant, possibly more deeply than they have known anyone in their lives, their knowledge often has a profound impact on them. The word *love* may describe this impact".[25] Phrased like that, it can take its place as a central aspect in the lives of Christian families.

Finally we come to empathy. We all know the importance of empathy and yet it is very easy in our daily lives to deny our children's feelings. On a simple level, we may not respond when they tell us they are hot or cold if the thermometer seems to suggest otherwise. On a more complicated level, children sometimes respond in unexpected ways to ordinary life events, especially if they have suffered early trauma. Adopted children often find a change of routine incredibly difficult, for instance, which can result in their having a meltdown on their birthday or at Christmas. On one level, they may want presents and attention but, on a deeper level, the change of routine can be unsettling as it takes them away from what is familiar and comfortable. In these situations we may well struggle to remain empathetic. However, as Dan Hughes writes, empathy "conveys to the infant that the parents are aware of his or her distress, will not leave him or her alone, and will help him or her to manage even if the distress does not stop".[26] It is essential for any healthy parent–child relationship.

Going at God's pace

So how do these insights help us in our relationship with God? If we are the adopted children of God, does he then parent us with a higher version of PACE? It is clear that our collective sense of awe before the majesty of God has

25 Hughes and Baylin, *Brain-Based Parenting*, 121.
26 Hughes and Baylin, *Brain-Based Parenting*, 130.

diminished in recent years. There has been an unfortunate tendency to think that we can cosy up to him, forgetting that coming before him with fear and trembling should be our default position. He is, after all, "the blessed and only Sovereign, the King of kings and Lord of lords. It is he alone who has immortality and dwells in unapproachable light, whom no one has ever seen or can see" (1 Timothy 6:15-16). Our country's recent rediscovery of the importance of Eucharistic Adoration is therefore an important corrective to the rather casual approach to God's presence that has permeated our lives and liturgies in recent years.

Nonetheless, we should not fall into the opposite error of seeing God as wholly unapproachable. "God so loved the world that he gave his only Son, so that everyone who believes in him may not perish but may have eternal life", as John tells us in his Gospel (John 3:16) before reiterating the point in his First Letter: "In this is love, not that we loved God but that he loved us and sent his Son to be the atoning sacrifice for our sins" (1 John 4:10). Having entered into the depths of our suffering, he has certainly not withdrawn into glorious isolation. We might know this on one level and yet still struggle to accept the notion of God's playfulness. However, if playfulness is "a frequent reciprocal attitude that occurs between the parent and the child", then we can certainly suggest that God is playful.[27] In fact, if we return to the Bible we could go even further and say that God's playfulness is an aspect of his sense of humour.

A common mistake that students make when writing about Jane Austen or Oscar Wilde in exam conditions is that they become far too solemn. Ignoring the wit that runs through Austen's novels and Wilde's plays, they can write as though the authors had no sense of humour at all. We can take the same approach to the scriptures. Consider the book of

27 Hughes and Baylin, *Brain-Based Parenting*, 105.

Jonah, for example. It would be easy to read the book and miss its humour, but surely the account is meant to be funny. From Jonah making the ludicrous decision to try to run away from God himself to the moment he left Nineveh in a sulk, the comic moments pile up. When God sent an enormous storm the sailors were so terrified that they each cried out to their own god and started throwing goods overboard; even so, Jonah managed to sleep through the chaos (despite the fact that even the ship itself threatened to break up). Then, of course, there is the comedy of being swallowed by a great fish, living for three days inside its belly and then suffering the indignity of being vomited onto dry land.

And the humour doesn't end there. When Jonah preached to the people of Nineveh, they repented with surprising swiftness, so much so that the king ordered not just the humans but even the animals to wear sackcloth as a sign of their repentance. The humour continues even after that comic turn. Jonah's temper tantrum in the last section of the story is also darkly comic. There we are assuming that the reason he ran away was that he was afraid, but the real reason is given only after the people of Nineveh have turned away from their sins: "O Lord! Is not this what I said while I was still in my own country? That is why I fled to Tarshish at the beginning; for I knew that you are a gracious God and merciful, slow to anger, and abounding in steadfast love, and ready to relent from punishing" (Jonah 4:2).

The story of Jonah is meant to be funny, but that doesn't mean that it can't also carry a serious message. "About what other subjects can one make jokes except serious subjects?", as G. K. Chesterton once asked.[28] Jonah's story is a powerful parable – in fact, it prefigures the parable of the prodigal son, even down to the sulking in the final part of the story – but parables can sometimes be told with a twinkle in the

28 G. K. Chesterton, *Heretics* (Thirsk: House of Stratus, 2001), 94.

eye. Just as we can enjoy reading, or hearing, them, God can enjoy telling them.

The truth is that God loves us as parents love their children. He delights in us and is playful with us. He likes telling us stories. We can too easily develop what has been called a hardening of the oughteries, focusing on the expectations we believe that God has of us rather than revelling in the unconditional love he showers upon us. However, God really is playful, he really accepts us, he really is curious about us and – having become one of us – he really has empathy with us too. That is why Blessed Columba Marmion, quoting St Leo the Great, could write in this beautiful way about our divine adoption:

> "The gift surpassing all gifts is that God calls a man His child, and that a man calls God his Father." Each one of us can say of himself or herself, in all truth: "It is by an individual act of love and kindness that God has created me and has called me, by baptism, to Divine adoption." For, in His plenitude and His infinite richness, God has no need of any creature: "*Of His own will* He has begotten us by the word of truth." By a special act of loving-kindness and fondness, God has chosen me – *elegit nos*, has chosen us – to be raised infinitely above my natural condition, to enjoy eternally His own beatitude, to be the realization of one of His Divine thoughts, to be one voice in the concert of the elect, to be one of those brethren who are like Jesus, and who share, without end, His celestial inheritance.[29]

29 Marmion, *Christ, the Life of the Soul*, 30-31.

[T]hen the Lord God formed man from the dust of the ground, and breathed into his nostrils the breath of life; and the man became a living being. And the Lord God planted a garden in Eden, in the east; and there he put the man whom he had formed. Out of the ground the Lord God made to grow every tree that is pleasant to the sight and good for food, the tree of life also in the midst of the garden, and the tree of the knowledge of good and evil. Genesis 2:7-9

Joseph also went from the town of Nazareth in Galilee to Judea, to the city of David called Bethlehem, because he was descended from the house and family of David. He went to be registered with Mary, to whom he was engaged and who was expecting a child. While they were there, the time came for her to deliver her child. And she gave birth to her firstborn son and wrapped him in bands of cloth, and laid him in a manger, because there was no place for them in the inn. Luke 2:4-7

Were Adam and Eve children?

How old were Adam and Eve? It may not be a question that often occurs to us. It might not seem like an important question either, but for one of the great Church Fathers it *was* an important question. Whereas most of the Church Fathers thought that Adam and Eve were created as perfect adults, St Irenaeus of Lyons believed that they were created as children and that the Fall of humanity can be explained in part as a desire to grow up too quickly.

St Irenaeus believed that Adam "was very little, for he was an infant, and it was necessary for him to reach full development by growing".[30] Just like us, Adam had to grow up. This is an idea that Irenaeus took further in *Adversus Haereses* ("Against the Heresies"), the most important of his books to have survived, writing that "it was necessary that man should in the first instance be created; and having been created, should receive growth; and having received growth, should be strengthened; and having been strengthened, should abound; and having abounded, should recover; and having recovered, should be glorified; and being glorified, should see his Lord".[31] Irenaeus knew his Bible very well. He knew that God had told Adam and Eve to be fruitful and multiply (Genesis 1:28), but he believed that they needed to attain maturity before they could do so: "in Paradise they were both naked, and were not ashamed, inasmuch as they, having been created a short time previously, had no understanding of the procreation of children: for it was necessary that they should first come to adult age, and then multiply from that time onward".[32]

30 Irenaeus, *Epideixis*, 12, quoted in Matthew Steenberg, *Irenaeus on Creation: the cosmic Christ and the saga of redemption* (Leiden: Brill, 2008), 142.

31 Irenaeus, *Against the Heresies*, 4.38.3. Available online at http://www.newadvent.org/fathers/0103.htm, accessed 29 Dec. 2018.

32 Irenaeus, *Against the Heresies*, 3.22.4.

This interpretation of the creation story raises all sorts of questions and suggests all kinds of intriguing possibilities. The first question is *why* God might have chosen to create Adam and Eve as children rather than as fully fledged adults. Irenaeus' argument was that, although all things are possible for God, anything created by God must, by definition, be inferior to him and so be in need of further development: "it was in the power of God Himself to grant perfection to man from the beginning; but the man, on the contrary, was unable to receive it, since he was still an infant".[33] Part of the purpose of God, in other words, was for Adam and Eve to grow up in the Garden of Eden, learning from God as he walked with them. What caused the Fall, therefore, was not so much pride as haste: the desire to grow up too quickly. The great twentieth-century theologian Hans Urs von Balthasar explains it this way:

> God intended man to have *all* good, but in his, God's time; and therefore all disobedience, all sin, consists essentially in breaking out of time. Hence the restoration of order by the Son of God had to be the annulment of that premature snatching at knowledge, the beating down of the hand outstretched towards eternity, the repentant return from a false, swift transfer into eternity to a true, slow confinement in time.[34]

The problem was not so much that Adam and Eve wanted knowledge but that they wanted it prematurely, that is to

33 Irenaeus, *Against the Heresies*, 4.38.1.
34 Hans Urs von Balthasar, *A Theology of History* (New York: Sheed and Ward, 1963), 30.

say before they were ready to be able to cope with it. As another writer put it, the "haste of sin is finally a desire for closure, a wish to be done with waiting... the desire no longer to be liable to the operation of another".[35] Adam and Eve just wanted to get on with it and, tempted by the snake, they decided that if God had other ideas then it must be God who'd got it wrong. Looking at it in this way, the traditional explanation that the Fall was down to Adam and Eve's pride, their desire to go it alone, actually ties in very well with Irenaeus' interpretation.

Irenaeus' interpretation may well also remind us of our own behaviour. How often do we wish that change would happen according to our timescales rather than God's? How often do we think that our prayers haven't been answered simply because they haven't been answered *when* we think they should have been? And how often do we wish our children would mature at a pace that fits in with our own requirements? The honest truth is that we too need to be reminded that God's ways are not our ways and God's timings are not our timings either.

Holy longing

So why is it that we have to wait? Why was Christ born so many years after the Fall? Why has the Second Coming still not happened two thousand years after the first coming of Jesus? St Augustine gave an answer to those questions in a homily on the First Letter of John:

> The whole life of the good Christian is a holy longing. What you long for, as yet you do not see; but longing

35 Jeff Vogel, "The Haste of Sin, the Slowness of Salvation: an interpretation of Irenaeus on the fall and redemption", *Anglican Theological Review*, 89 (3) (2007), 448.

> makes in you the room that shall be filled, when that which you are to see shall come. When you would fill a purse, knowing how large a present it is to hold, you stretch wide its cloth or leather; knowing how much you are to put in it, and seeing that the purse is small, you extend it to make more room. So by withholding the vision God extends the longing, through longing he makes the soul extend, by extending it he makes more room in it. So, brethren, let us long, because we are to be filled.[36]

It is only when we are ready to receive God that we will receive him. Though God always makes the first move, we have to be capable of receiving him and that capability comes by means of a holy yearning. This might sound daunting but we can rephrase the same point, saying that it is only when we are at our lowest ebb that we really yearn for God. It is only when we are at the end of our tether, when nothing seems to be going right, when our lives and our children seem out of our control that we stop trying to get by in our own strength and really reach out to God. It is only then that God is able to fill us with his fullness.

One of my favourite prayers is the Salve Regina, which makes no bones about the fact that we are "poor banished children of Eve" and that we are currently in "exile". Exile in the ancient world was often seen as a punishment worse than death. Being cut off from home without any prospect of an immediate return was a fate that poets bewailed and philosophers refused to face. Being banished provoked an intense yearning for return. That is why, "mourning and weeping in this vale of tears", we send up our sighs

36 St Augustine, *Augustine: later works* (Westminster: John Knox Press, 1955), 290.

to Our Lady. We really are lost and, in the Salve Regina, we acknowledge it in heartfelt terms. But – and this is the important point – we are not simply complaining when we pray in this way, nor are we bemoaning our lot: we are expressing our yearning that "we may be made worthy of the promises of Christ", knowing that being made worthy will take time, but knowing too that when we truly yearn for God he will not turn away from us.

Summing up in Christ

This digression on the importance of waiting brings us back to Irenaeus and childhood: not just Adam and Eve's but Jesus'. Irenaeus explained that:

> God had power at the beginning to grant perfection to man; but as the latter was only recently created, he could not possibly have received it, or even if he had received it, could he have contained it, or containing it, could he have retained it. It was for this reason that the Son of God, although He was perfect, passed through the state of infancy in common with the rest of mankind, partaking of it thus not for His own benefit, but for that of the infantile stage of man's existence, in order that man might be able to receive Him.[37]

What we have here is an answer to another basic, but crucial, question: why was Jesus born as a baby at all? Why could he not have appeared on earth as a fully formed adult? This question takes us right to the heart of the passages

37 Irenaeus, *Against the Heresies*, 4.38.2.

we have been focusing on in this book. Since the Gospels focus primarily on the public ministry of Christ – on just three years of Jesus' life – we might well wonder what the point was of his first thirty years, those hidden years when he was growing up in Nazareth.

The answer that Irenaeus gives is that, in order to save us, Christ, the second Adam, had to undo the damage that had been done by the first Adam. That meant that he had to relive the life of Adam in a perfect way. Instead of Adam's disobedience, Jesus was perfectly obedient to God the Father. Adam was tempted in a garden, so Jesus withstood temptation in the Garden of Gethsemane. Adam fell because he ate from a tree: Jesus brought us back to God by dying on a tree. Following St Paul, the word that Irenaeus uses for this redemptive work is recapitulation, which means summing up.[38] Irenaeus' teaching about recapitulation is fascinating but complex, so much so that one critic has claimed that the concept contains at least eleven ideas.[39] You will be relieved to hear that I am going to concentrate only on what the notion of recapitulation can tell us about the childhoods of Adam, Eve and Jesus.

Irenaeus argued that it wasn't simply as an adult that Jesus recapitulated the life of Adam but also as a child:

> He therefore passed through every age, becoming an infant for infants, thus sanctifying infants; a child for children, thus sanctifying those who are of this age, being at the same time made to them an example of piety, righteousness, and submission; a youth for

38 The word appears in Ephesians 1:10, though it is often translated as "unite" rather than "recapitulate", which is the more precise translation.

39 Eric Osborn, *Irenaeus of Lyon* (Cambridge: Cambridge University Press, 2001), 97.

> youths, becoming an example to youths, and thus sanctifying them for the Lord.[40]

This was not simply a case of digitally remastering a film that was in a terrible state of repair – "Adam, the Movie" remade as "Jesus, the Movie" – because there was a clear reason why Jesus had to be born, grow and become the perfect adult he did:

> And for this cause our Lord in these last times, when He had summed up all things into Himself, came to us, not as He might have come, but as we were capable of beholding Him. He might easily have come to us in His immortal glory, but in that case we could never have endured the greatness of the glory; and therefore it was that He, who was the perfect bread of the Father, offered Himself to us as milk.[41]

It would have been entirely possible for Jesus to appear in clouds of glory but, even with thousands of years of preparation, we still would not have been ready to receive him. Instead, he came as a baby who grew into a child who became an adult, so that he could recapitulate the life and growth of Adam – who must therefore also once have been a child in Irenaeus' estimation – and also so that he could give the people to whom he came the time they needed to receive the great gift that was God himself.

---

40 Irenaeus, *Against the Heresies*, 2.22.4.
41 Irenaeus, *Against the Heresies*, 4.38.1.

There is something powerfully symbolic about the Lord of life being born in a manger in anticipation of the fact that he would become the food that gives us life in the Holy Mass, but Irenaeus developed that symbolism in a novel way, writing that the perfect bread of the Father offered himself to us as milk "so that we, being nourished, as it were, from the breast of His flesh, and from such a course of nourishment becoming accustomed to eat and drink the Word of God, might be able to contain in ourselves Him who is the bread of immortality: the Spirit of the Father".[42] In other words, Christ's gift of himself was so amazing, so far beyond our wildest expectations, that we had to be weaned onto him first.

What we see, then, is that the question of whether Adam and Eve were children is not merely idle speculation on the part of a long-dead theologian. It is tied up with the more obviously striking question of why Jesus should have been born as a baby and, following on from that, it leads to the question of how we can receive him into our lives and families today. If we are children of God it is because Jesus, the Son of God, was a child first. If we are children of God then we need to be humble enough to accept that we need to be weaned on the "perfect bread of the Father [who] offered Himself to us as milk". If we are children of God then we don't need to rush to grow up.

The child Moses

With all this in mind, we can take another look at our Bibles, seeing patterns that we might not have noticed before. A simple but striking feature of the Old Testament is how often we hear about the childhood of some of the most important people in salvation history. The most well-known example is Moses, who was hidden away for the first three months

42 Irenaeus, *Against the Heresies*, 4.38.1.

of his life – just as Jesus later had to be hidden away in Egypt by his parents – to save him from the cruelty of an unjust ruler. Already we can see that this story has a wider resonance, foreshadowing the life and work of Jesus, but to understand the story fully we need to look backwards as well as forwards. Exquisitely turning Pharaoh's words against him, Moses' mother obeyed his order – "every boy that is born to the Hebrews you shall throw into the Nile" (Exodus 1:22) – by taking "a papyrus basket for [her son], and plaster[ing] it with bitumen and pitch" (Exodus 2:3) before putting the child in it and setting it down on the river. The little details are important here. We are meant to remember another story about an object being covered with pitch before floating away on the water. Noah's ark may have been built on a far greater scale than Moses' basket but it did essentially the same work: saving its inhabitants from destruction so they could bring greater glory to God.

Another tiny detail in the story reaches out to us across the years: we are told that when Pharaoh's daughter opened Moses' basket, the child "was crying" (Exodus 2:6). Given the circumstances, this is hardly surprising. What is surprising, though, is that this apparently inconsequential detail should have found its way into the narrative, the book of Exodus being an account of God's mighty works. Exodus cries out for epic treatment: so many events in the book are hugely dramatic. But we start with just ten verses about the childhood of Moses and one of those verses tells us that he was crying. What we learn from this moving passage is that nothing is inconsequential to God, not even the pitiful cries of a young child, a message that Jesus was powerfully to reinforce, not just by being born as a baby himself but also by telling his followers that not a sparrow falls to the ground without the Father knowing about it (Luke 12:6-7).

The greatness of God does not preclude an interest in every tiny detail of his creation.

The other message that comes through loud and clear in this story is that the power of God works through people's weakness. Pharaoh thought he was almighty but he turned out to have very little power at all. Moses seemed to be wholly unimportant but he turned out to be one of the greatest leaders ever to have lived.

Samuel and David

Moses was not the only person whose childhood we hear about in the Old Testament. We have already seen how Samuel's story prefigures the story of Jesus, but the story of Samuel did not end with his childhood. As an adult, he was called upon to choose a new king for Israel and, much to his surprise, God led him not to the rich and powerful but to the young and overlooked. Having travelled to Bethlehem to choose a king from among Jesse's sons, Samuel did what everyone would have expected of him by looking first to Eliab, the eldest son. Given his own calling, Samuel should perhaps have realised that God's expectations were unlikely to match those of his people: "Do not look on his appearance", God told him, "or on the height of his stature, because I have rejected him; for the Lord does not see as mortals see; they look on the outward appearance, but the Lord looks on the heart" (1 Samuel 16:7). Not seeing the heart, Jesse had failed to present David to Samuel because he was "the youngest, but he is keeping the sheep" (1 Samuel 16:11). But it really was the youngest whom God wanted. It was David whom Samuel eventually chose as king.

Just as with Moses, it was the one who was chosen as a child who delivered his people from their enemies. Just as with Moses, it was the one who seemed weakest of all who turned out to be the strongest. When Goliath challenged the Israelites to single combat, "Saul and all Israel... were dismayed and greatly afraid" (1 Samuel 17:11). David, however, was undaunted, asking "[W]ho is this uncircumcised Philistine that he should defy the armies of the living God?" (1 Samuel 17:26). To hammer home the point that this was God's fight and not his, David refused Saul's offer of a bronze helmet and a coat of mail, taking his staff, his sling and five smooth stones from the brook instead. What follows is another masterly passage of descriptive writing, a vignette that makes a profoundly important theological point through a highly memorable story:

> The Philistine said to David, "Am I a dog, that you come to me with sticks?" And the Philistine cursed David by his gods. The Philistine said to David, "Come to me, and I will give your flesh to the birds of the air and to the wild animals of the field." But David said to the Philistine, "You come to me with sword and spear and javelin; but I come to you in the name of the Lord of hosts, the God of the armies of Israel, whom you have defied. This very day the Lord will deliver you into my hand, and I will strike you down and cut off your head; and I will give the dead bodies of the Philistine army this very day to the birds of the air and to the wild animals of the earth, so that all the earth may know that there is a God in Israel, and that all this assembly may know that the Lord does not save by sword and spear; for the battle is the Lord's and he will give you into our hand." **(1 Samuel 17:43-47)**

Throughout salvation history, God chose the weak and the powerless to do his mighty works. It might be of some consolation and encouragement in the ordinariness of our lives to remember that he continues to do so today.

The wonder of childhood

It may not, ultimately, be important whether Adam and Eve were children or not, but St Irenaeus' argument certainly opens a fruitful line of enquiry, reminding us of the many references in the scriptures to children and childhood. By linking recapitulation with childhood, he also created a way for Christians in the twenty-first century to respond to the frenetic age in which we find ourselves. To demonstrate how Irenaeus' ideas can make sense in the modern age, we can usefully turn to two great, but contrasting, figures from the twentieth century: G. K. Chesterton and Hans Urs von Balthasar.

In a wonderful chapter on "The Ethics of Elfland" from *Orthodoxy*, his great comic defence of Christian belief, Chesterton draws our attention to the vital importance of wonder:

> A child of seven is excited by being told that Tommy opened a door and saw a dragon. But a child of three is excited by being told that Tommy opened a door... nursery tales only echo an almost pre-natal leap of interest and amazement. These tales say that apples are golden only to refresh the forgotten moment when we found that they were green. They make rivers run with wine only to make us remember, for one wild moment, that they run with water.[43]

43 G. K. Chesterton, *Orthodoxy* (London: Fontana, 1961), 52-53.

He then adds:

> The test of all happiness is gratitude; and I felt grateful, though I hardly knew to whom. Children are grateful when Santa Claus puts in their stockings gifts of toys or sweets. Could I not be grateful to Santa Claus when he put in my stockings the gift of two miraculous legs? We thank people for birthday presents of cigars and slippers. Can I thank no one for the birthday present of birth?[44]

This sense of wonder was important for von Balthasar as well. As he explained in one of his last books, Jesus "retained all the traits of the child of God even as he was entrusted with the difficult, superhuman task of leading the whole world back home to God".[45] Chief among these traits was a sense of "eternal childlike amazement: 'The Father is greater than I' (Jn 14: 28)".[46] This sense of amazement, for von Balthasar, was at the very heart of the Son's relationship with his Father, not just during his time as a child on earth but throughout all eternity:

> We can be sure that the human Child Jesus was in amazement over everything: beginning with the existence of his loving Mother, then passing on to his own existence, finally going from both to all the forms offered by the surrounding world, from the tiniest flower to the boundless skies. But this amazement

44 Chesterton, *Orthodoxy*, 53-54.
45 Hans Urs von Balthasar, *Unless You Become Like this Child* (San Francisco: Ignatius Press, 1991), 44.
46 von Balthasar, *Unless You Become Like this Child*, 44.

derives from the much deeper amazement of the eternal Child who, in the absolute Spirit of Love, marvels at Love itself as it permeates and transcends all that is.[47]

Having established the importance of amazement, von Balthasar then asked the questions that every parent and teacher must have considered: why is it that children lose their initial sense of wonder and how can it be retained? Unusually, he lays the blame in part at the door of the education system, which draws children away from their natural sense of amazement and wonder; less controversially, he also focuses on the impact of technology on children's perception of the world:

> Childlike amazement is not easy to preserve since so much in education aims at learning habits, mastering tasks and grasping automatic functions. Technology (think of all the electronic toys for children) only adds a new dimension to this delight in mastering things.[48]

If education and technology are the root causes of our loss of wonder, then the answer to this fundamental problem is a total rethinking of our relationship with time: "The child has time to take time as it comes, one day at a time, calmly,

47 von Balthasar, *Unless You Become Like this Child*, 46.
48 von Balthasar, *Unless You Become Like this Child*, 46.

without advance planning or greedy hoarding of time. Time to play, time to sleep. He knows nothing of appointment books in which every moment has already been sold in advance."[49] By contrast, "[p]ressured man on the run is always postponing his encounter with God to a 'free moment' or a 'time of prayer' that must constantly be rescheduled, a time that he must laboriously wrest from his overburdened workday".[50] What all of us need, then, is a childlike sense of time, an ability to take our time by taking time as it comes.

This focus on taking our time may well remind us of the Slow Movement, whose greatest contribution in the last few decades has been its reappraisal of time. When Carlo Petrini called for a Slow Food movement, he wasn't suggesting that we all buy slow cookers and chew more: he was arguing that the production and consumption of food had become divorced from the natural world on which it remained utterly dependent. The essence of the Slow Movement, in other words, is not going slowly but finding the right pace. In a similar way, the slowness of salvation is not so much a matter of slowness as a matter of working at God's pace, accepting that he always acts in what the Bible calls "the fullness of time". When we accept God's time, God's timings and God's pace, we find that our own relationship with time is restored. What had become disordered is reordered. What had slipped out of joint is restored. The world is made right again.

---

49 von Balthasar, *Unless You Become Like this Child*, 53-54.
50 von Balthasar, *Unless You Become Like this Child*, 54-55.

III

Education

About the middle of the festival Jesus went up into the temple and began to teach. The Jews were astonished at it, saying, "How does this man have such learning, when he has never been taught?" Then Jesus answered them, "My teaching is not mine but his who sent me. Anyone who resolves to do the will of God will know whether the teaching is from God or whether I am speaking on my own. Those who speak on their own seek their own glory; but the one who seeks the glory of him who sent him is true, and there is nothing false in him." John 7:14-18

Now when they saw the boldness of Peter and John and realized that they were uneducated and ordinary men, they were amazed and recognized them as companions of Jesus. Acts 4:13

Where is the one who is wise? Where is the scribe? Where is the debater of this age? Has not God made foolish the wisdom of the world? For since, in the wisdom of God, the world did not know God through wisdom, God decided, through the foolishness of our proclamation, to save those who believe. For Jews demand signs and Greeks desire wisdom, but we proclaim Christ crucified, a stumbling-block to Jews and foolishness to Gentiles, but to those who are the called, both Jews and Greeks, Christ the power of God and the wisdom of God. For God's foolishness is wiser than human wisdom, and God's weakness is stronger than human strength. 1 Corinthians 1:20-25

Did Jesus go to school?

Considering the huge amount of research that has been carried out into the life of Jesus, we might think that it would be easy to find out whether Jesus went to school, but it isn't. The essential difficulty is that we have very little information about Jewish education in Nazareth at the time of Jesus. We know quite a lot about Jewish education in the period *after* the destruction of the Temple in AD 70, but there is very little hard evidence of the period before that. What tends to happen, therefore, is that writers who are anxious to fill in the gaps in Jesus' hidden life read information and assumptions back into his time, creating an illusion of certainty where no such certainty exists.

It has sometimes been assumed, for example, that, because Jesus began his public ministry by visiting the synagogue in Nazareth on the sabbath and reading from the book of the prophet Isaiah, he must have gone to school. The importance of Mary, Joseph and education in the home is ignored altogether. Other readings of the evidence that are more sophisticated can still fall into the trap of reading the present into the past. One author, for example, develops an interesting interpretation of Jesus' early life before drifting into strange anachronisms, telling us that Joseph's family was "middle class" and, even more surprisingly, that Jesus' "students ... followed him day and night for three years in his mobile Bible school".[1] We may never establish the truth with any complete degree of assurance, but we can certainly examine the evidence and see where it leads us.

Until comparatively recently, many scholars argued that Jesus probably did go to school, studying at his local synagogue as other boys of his age would have done. According to this line of argument, "education started at

1 Göran Lennartsson, "Jesus' Training & Pentecostal Education Today", *Journal of the European Pentecostal Theological Association*, 32 (2) (2012), 146.

the age of five or six and continued for five years. In this elementary (*bet sefer*) level boys in classes of twenty-five studied the Bible. Portions were memorized each day, and reading as well as writing ability was practised".[2] Jesus' education, in other words, was firmly rooted in the scriptures, which is why he developed the ability to read and write. What is less clear in this tradition of historical writing is what happened next. Boys could study for a further five years and even study at an advanced level in Jerusalem but it certainly wasn't a universal requirement, so it is difficult to see how Jesus, coming from a poor family, could possibly have afforded such an education. On the other hand, he clearly taught with authority and was more than capable of holding his own in debate with the Pharisees and Sadducees, which could suggest that his theological training was considerably more advanced than that of most carpenters' sons.

There are several problems with these historical reconstructions of Jesus' early years, however. Firstly, they fail to take the extraordinary nature of Jesus into account. As the Son of God who had to be in his Father's house at the age of twelve, he did not necessarily require a formal theological training to develop the knowledge and wisdom he clearly had in abundance. Secondly, they fail to take into account the deep education that Jesus would have received from his earthly parents. If Mary and Joseph were the most remarkable parents who ever lived then it surely follows that the education they would have provided in the everyday course of events would have been extraordinary too. What need did Jesus have of another teacher when he had Mary as his mother? Thirdly, conventional accounts of Jesus' schooling also fall into the trap of reading historical facts back into an earlier period. We know from Simeon ben Shetach in about 100 BC that all boys were expected to go to

2 Lennartsson, "Jesus' Training", 142.

school but we have no evidence that this actually happened, least of all in Nazareth, which was far from being the cultural hub of ancient Israel.[3] What evidence we do have comes from much later, after the time of Jesus.

Catherine Hezser, Professor of Jewish Studies at SOAS, University of London, has cast doubt on the neat image that many previous writers worked with, pointing out that:

> [t]he traditional assumption of an organized system of Jewish primary education in Hellenistic and Roman times which would have been supplemented by hierarchically organized and centrally controlled rabbinic academies of higher learning after 70 CE has been repudiated by more critical and methodologically sophisticated studies in recent years.[4]

Despite extensive archaeological work, no schools or academies have yet been excavated, which suggests that an organised system of primary education was more an aspiration than a reality. What's more, "the large majority of Jews, especially those who lived in the rural areas of Galilee, would not have had sufficient leisure time and money to engage in any type of learning besides the practical skills needed for subsistence farming and small-scale business".[5] Hezser argues that "neither the Hebrew Bible, nor the New

3 Alan Millard, *Reading and Writing in the Time of* Jesus (Sheffield: Sheffield Academic Press, 2001), 157.

4 Catherine Hezser, "Private and Public Education", in Catherine Hezser (ed.), *The Oxford Handbook of Jewish Daily Life in Roman Palestine* (Oxford: OUP, 2010), 465.

5 Catherine Hezser, "The Torah Versus Homer: Jewish and Greco-Roman Education in Late Roman Palestine", in Matthew Ryan Hauge and Andrew W. Pitts (eds.), *Ancient Education and Early Christianity* (London: Bloomsbury, 2016), 5.

Testament, or any of the Jewish writings of the Second Temple period, including Philo and Josephus, contain any direct references to schools for the primary education of Jewish children"[6] and approvingly quotes another scholar who claimed that "to the mass of people the concept of education, of teaching and learning as a continuous process unconnected with immediate practical needs, hardly existed in earlier times".[7]

What we have here, in other words, is a category error. As another scholar suggests, to speak about school in the sense that we think of it today "is often meaningless in the ancient world".[8] In the ancient world, what school meant, in effect, was "the activity carried on rather than... the person teaching, the student-teacher relationship, or the premises where teaching takes place. The teacher could be a friend, a parent, a priest, or someone hired to teach, and the classroom a room in a private house, the shaded porch of a temple, or the dusty ground under a tree".[9] If Jesus went to school, it certainly was not a school in the sense that we understand the word today, and if he had formal schooling of any kind there is certainly no evidence of it in the Gospels, in contemporary written documents or in the archaeological record.

The education of Jesus

So what does the Bible suggest about the education of Jesus? An important verse in John's Gospel tells us about the time when Jesus went up into the Temple and started teaching. That someone like him should be teaching in the

6 Hezser, "Private and Public Education", 470.
7 Hezser, "Private and Public Education", 470.
8 Raffaella Cribiore, *Writing, Teachers, and Students in Graeco-Roman Egypt* (Atlanta, Georgia: Scholars Press, 1996), 6.
9 Cribiore, *Writing, Teachers, and Students*, 6.

Temple of all places amazed many of his hearers, prompting them to ask: "How does this man have such learning, when he has never been taught?" (John 7:15). On the face of it, this question strongly suggests that Jesus was not formally trained as a rabbi and may well not have been formally educated at all.

A parallel passage is to be found in the Acts of the Apostles, where Luke tells us that when the Jewish authorities "saw the boldness of Peter and John and realized that they were uneducated and ordinary men, they were amazed and recognized them as companions of Jesus" (Acts 4:13). In both cases, the power of the message comes precisely from the fact that Jesus and his disciples were not well educated, or at least from the fact that they were not formally educated. Their message was, therefore, all the more powerful because it came directly from God. Jesus explained that "my teaching is not mine, but his who sent me" (John 7:16), while Peter and John revelled in the fact that "we cannot keep from speaking about what we have seen and heard" (Acts 4:20), by which they meant what they had heard from Jesus and seen him do. That does not necessarily mean that they were wholly uneducated, as the Jewish authorities rather dismissively suggested, but it does suggest that they had not received a formal theological education.

St Paul developed this insight on several occasions in his letters. Even though he studied "at the feet of Gamaliel" and was "educated strictly according to our ancestral law" (Acts 22:3), he knew that his formal education counted for very little in the eyes of God. As he explained to the Corinthians:

> Christ did not send me to baptize but to proclaim the gospel, and not with eloquent wisdom, so that the cross of Christ might not be emptied of its power. For the message about the cross is foolishness to those who are perishing, but to us who are being saved it is the power of God. For it is written, "I will destroy the wisdom of the wise, and the discernment of the discerning I will thwart." **1 Corinthians 1:17-19**

This idea was clearly very important to St Paul since he developed it over several more paragraphs, asking a series of rhetorical questions – "Where is the one who is wise? Where is the scribe? Where is the debater of this age? Has not God made foolish the wisdom of the world?" – before arguing that "God's foolishness is wiser than human wisdom, and God's weakness is stronger than human strength"(1 Corinthians 1:20-25).

He also explained why God chose the weak and powerless, arguing that:

> God chose what is foolish in the world to shame the wise; God chose what is weak in the world to shame the strong; God chose what is low and despised in the world, things that are not, to reduce to nothing things that are, so that no one might boast in the presence of God. He is the source of your life in Christ Jesus, who became for us wisdom from God, and

> righteousness and sanctification and redemption, in order that, as it is written, "Let the one who boasts, boast in the Lord." **1 Corinthians 1:27-31**

If Christ is our wisdom and if God's foolishness is wiser than human wisdom, there was no good reason why Jesus should have gone to school. If wisdom – God's wisdom – is the goal of education, then having formal schooling isn't the be-all and end-all of education.

Jesus, the carpenter's son

So, if Jesus didn't go to school – or if, at least, we cannot be certain that he went to school – what did he learn at home? A good starting point for any such discussion is St John Paul II's argument in *Redemptoris Custos* ("The Custodian of the Redeemer") about the importance of work:

> Work was the daily expression of love in the life of the Family of Nazareth. The Gospel specifies the kind of work Joseph did in order to support his family: he was a carpenter. This simple word sums up Joseph's entire life. For Jesus, these were hidden years, the years to which Luke refers after recounting the episode that occurred in the Temple: "And he went down with them and came to Nazareth, and was obedient to them" (Lk 2:51). This "submission" or obedience of Jesus in the house of Nazareth should be understood as a sharing in the work of Joseph. Having learned the work of his presumed father, he was known as "the carpenter's son." If the Family of Nazareth is an

> example and model for human families, in the order of salvation and holiness, so too, by analogy, is Jesus' work at the side of Joseph the carpenter.[10]

Jesus learned from St Joseph by working with him. His education was not simply an education in the word of God, though it was certainly that; it was also an education in how to work wood. As Fabrice Hadjadj has reminded us, God the Father sent Jesus not by "brandishing lightning bolts direct from the sky" nor by "having him deliver sermons from his mother's breast" but "by making him a carpenter".[11]

This is a point to which we must constantly return, as long as we remember that being a carpenter in Jesus' day was not necessarily the same as it is now, when "wood-working is done with machine production and computerization in mind".[12] Jesus learned from St Joseph to work with the wood, and how to work with people too. He learned not at the feet of his master but at his side. As an apprentice, he learned not so much from St Joseph's words as from his actions, and not so much from his actions as from that silence in which St Joseph lived his hidden life with God.

There is an important sense in which Jesus' education was a home education. Whether or not he studied in a school attached to a synagogue, he certainly spent years learning from his parents in their home. When Luke tells us that Jesus came to Nazareth and was obedient to Mary and Joseph, he really means it. However, it is also worth pointing

10 St John Paul II, *Redemptoris Custos* ("Guardian of the Redeemer), 22.

11 Fabrice Hadjadj, *Résurrection mode d'emploi* (Paris: Magnificat, 2016), 135. Translated as *Experience Life in the Risen Christ*.

12 Fabrice Hadjadj, "Rediscovering the 'Language of Wood': why can't we just substitute 'be fruitful and multiply' with 'connect and download'", Humanum Review Website (2015). http://humanumreview.com/articles/rediscovering-the-language-of-wood-why-cant-we-just-substitute-be-fruitful-and-multiply-with-connect-and-download, accessed 28 Dec. 2018.

out that if "school" as we understand the word today is something of an anachronism when applied to the world in which Jesus lived, it is also true that "home education" as it is usually understood today is also an anachronism. In the twenty-first century, choosing to educate your children at home is always also a decision *not* to have them educated at school. In Jesus' day, this was not the case. The normal state of affairs was for children to learn from their parents, with no strict distinction being made between academic and practical learning. What is more, the education that was given in the home was always supplemented by – or clearly integrated with – an education in the sacred scriptures that would have taken place in the synagogue as the family joined other families for worship. Education took place in the home but home was not insulated from the wider family or from the local community. As we have already seen, when Jesus went missing at the age of twelve, the first place his parents looked was among their relatives since they were all on pilgrimage together.

Hillside reveries

The Holy Family would have been keenly aware of the wider world. Living in first-century Israel, they would have had a deep sense of the broad national and international history that their nation had experienced through the centuries. They would also have been well aware of the continuing impact of this wider world on their daily lives. From the arrival of the Magi to the flight into Egypt to the obvious presence of Roman soldiers, they would have seen the wider world on their very doorstep. The impact of this broader environment was explored in a little book called *The Education of Christ: hillside reveries* written by William Ramsay, a Scottish biblical scholar, at the turn of the twentieth century. Ramsay's argument was that the place in which Jesus was raised was of fundamental importance in his education. Most of us would struggle to place many of the towns mentioned in the New Testament on a map, let alone have any sense of how they related to each other or to key stories from the Old Testament, but Ramsay argues that Jesus would have been brought up with a vivid awareness of the historical and religious significance of the places around him:

> No education was ever so well adapted to train a thoughtful child in the appreciation of his own country, to render its past history living and real to him, to strengthen his patriotic feeling, to make every geographical name and scene full of meaning and historic truth, as the training which every Hebrew child then received. He learned to know one small collection of books thoroughly, and that library gave him a training in literature and in history, in philosophic insight and in religious feeling.[13]

Jesus' education was an education in place, as well as an education at the carpenter's workbench and an education in the sacred scriptures. Or, to be more precise, Jesus' education was seamless: St Joseph taught him to work wood and to pray; the places he read about in the Bible were the places he knew; when he went to the synagogue he continued to learn with his family. Since modern education tends to fragment knowledge, splitting the wonderful wholeness of God's creation into separate subjects, and separate subjects

13 William Ramsay, *The Education of Christ: hillside reveries* (London: Hodder & Stoughton, 1902), 61-62.

into gobbets of testable information, we could do a lot worse than return to the educational simplicity that Jesus experienced. To put it simply, there is no evidence that Mary and Joseph ever organised extra tutoring in maths or Aramaic. In fact, there's absolutely no evidence that Jesus ever had a maths lesson. What is far more likely is that he picked up what mathematical knowledge he needed from St Joseph through working on particular practical projects. And not just maths: Jesus also got along just fine without science or football, without email or end-of-term tests.

To point out these facts is not to promote mindless technophobia. Rather, it is a reminder that we can get so caught up in the overwhelming morass of educational material that comes our way that we completely lose sight of what education is for. What Jesus knew – what he learned from Mary and Joseph – is that the goal of education is the love of God. Knowledge is not, strictly speaking, its own end. All truth points to Truth himself, just as all goodness and beauty point us towards God himself, the giver of all good and beautiful things. We may pass GCSEs, A Levels and degrees but still lack wisdom. We may end up with lots of letters after our name but never come to know God. We may know very little about Jesus' childhood, but we know for certain that in his father's house and workshop, in the synagogue in Nazareth and the Temple in Jerusalem, he never lost sight of the true end of education: to know and love God. That is what really matters, not where his or our children's education takes place.

Jesus went throughout Galilee, teaching in their synagogues and proclaiming the good news of the kingdom and curing every disease and every sickness among the people. So his fame spread throughout all Syria, and they brought to him all the sick, those who were afflicted with various diseases and pains, demoniacs, epileptics, and paralytics, and he cured them. And great crowds followed him from Galilee, the Decapolis, Jerusalem, Judea, and from beyond the Jordan.
When Jesus saw the crowds, he went up the mountain; and after he sat down, his disciples came to him. Then he began to speak, and taught them, saying: "Blessed are the poor in spirit, for theirs is the kingdom of heaven." Matthew 4:23 – 5:3

Then he said to them, "Oh, how foolish you are, and how slow of heart to believe all that the prophets have declared! Was it not necessary that the Messiah should suffer these things and then enter into his glory?" Then beginning with Moses and all the prophets, he interpreted to them the things about himself in all the scriptures. Luke 24:25-27

How did Jesus teach?

Before we look at how Jesus taught, it might be worth considering what he *didn't* do. He never wrote a book. He never taught in a classroom. He didn't use blackboards or whiteboards or PowerPoint presentations. He didn't mark his disciples' work or give them end-of-unit tests. He wasn't a GCSE examiner, he didn't attend educational conferences and he didn't go to staff meetings. But, for all that, he was most definitely a teacher.

When we think about our own teachers, we remember their idiosyncrasies, what set them apart from the mainstream for good or for ill. In my case, I remember not just a long list of inspiring English teachers but also a great French teacher who taught, and dressed, with military discipline. Sporting a handlebar moustache and always wearing immaculately polished shoes, he expected high standards and he got them. By contrast, I had a teacher when studying Latin A Level at the girls' school across the road – our boys' school not offering such an esoteric subject for A Level – who used to disappear halfway through lessons and not always return. In his youth he had been a communist activist in South Africa during the apartheid era but when he taught us he was nearing retirement and his mind was usually on other things.

Those teachers have remained long in the memory but I don't remember my geography teachers at all, having given the subject up at the end of my second year of secondary school. However, I was fortunate enough to return to the subject when I moved to the Lake District for my first teaching job. Determined to learn more about the region in which I now lived, I studied for a postgraduate diploma in Lake District Studies at Lancaster University. There were some wonderful teachers on the course, all of whom taught like geography teachers even when their subjects were actually history or botany or literature. Once a week I drove down the M6 to Lancaster in my 2CV for an evening of lectures or seminars, but every few weeks we would head off on field trips to different parts of the Lake District. That is how I really got to know the place where I now lived, by studying botany on Scout Scar, by looking at glaciation in the Duddon Valley, by studying industrial archaeology in Borrowdale. I learned from teachers whose classroom was the Lake District itself. I learned through the soles of my feet.[14]

In a sense, Jesus taught like a geography teacher for he too was peripatetic, an itinerant teacher who never settled for long in one place. This is such a familiar aspect of his teaching style that we rarely ask ourselves why he should have chosen to teach in this way, when he could, in theory, have established himself in one particular place, whether that was the Temple in Jerusalem or a one-horse *dorp* in Galilee. Of course, he wasn't a geography teacher. His reason for getting out into the field was not to take a closer look at the local geology or to study the impact of tectonic activity on the mountains of Israel. The places where he taught were full of historical and religious meaning, but he travelled primarily as a good shepherd does, going out in search of lost sheep. He was rooted in one place for almost thirty years – after a brief stint as a refugee in Egypt – but he knew that the lost sheep of Israel would not be able to find their way back to him without help. He had to go in search of them.

Jesus was an itinerant teacher rather than a geography teacher, but that doesn't mean that the physical world was unimportant to him. Meeting a blind man by the roadside, "he spat on the ground and made mud with the saliva and spread the mud on the man's eyes" before telling him to wash in the pool of Siloam (John 9:6-7). This was an important passage for St Irenaeus, who argued that by curing the blind

14 Kieran O'Mahony, *Geography and Education: through the souls of our feet* (Seattle, WA: EduCare Press, 1988).

man with mud and saliva Jesus was teaching that it was he who first formed Adam from the mud of earth and he too who washes us clean in baptism to undo the fault of Adam.[15]

Mud mattered to Jesus but so too did mountains. He went up a mountain to pray, he chose his disciples on a mountain and the transfiguration took place on a mountain. Mountains mattered to Jesus but not in the same way that they matter to us today. He went up the mountain to pray, not to see the view. He went higher in order to spend time with his Father, not to conquer an untamed peak. He delivered the Sermon on the Mount as the new Moses, and that meant that he was claiming the highest teaching authority for himself:

> Jesus sits on the cathedra of Moses. But he does so not after the manner of teachers who trained for the job in a school; he sits there as the greater Moses, who broadens the Covenant to include all nations. This also explains the significance of the mountain. The Evangelist does not tell us which of the hills of Galilee it was. But the very fact that it is the scene of Jesus' preaching makes it simply "the mountain" – the new Sinai. The "mountain" is the place where Jesus prays – where he is face-to-face with the Father. And that is exactly why it is also the place of his teaching, since his teaching comes forth from this most intimate exchange with the Father.[16]

---

15 Irenaeus, *Against Heresies*, 15.4.

16 Joseph Ratzinger, *Jesus of Nazareth: from the baptism in the Jordan to the transfiguration* (London: Bloomsbury, 2007), 66.

Jesus travelled to find the lost sheep of Israel but some of the lost sheep also travelled with him. Why? Why did they have to accompany Jesus for three years to learn what he had to teach them? Why did they have to give up everything to go and follow him? To answer those questions, we need to leave mud and mountains behind for the time being and get to grips with the parables.

Revealing a mystery

Instead of imagining Jesus as a geography teacher, maybe we should rather picture him as a storyteller, a rabbi whose message was conveyed by means of his parables. The only problem with that idea is that we may not be entirely clear about what parables are. We bandy the word about but, since the parable is not a literary genre we are ever likely to find on the shelves of our local bookshop, we may not be absolutely certain what their purpose or nature is. In the second of his *Jesus of Nazareth* books, Pope Benedict XVI sketched out the beginnings of an answer, explaining that "the Hebrew word *mashal* (parable, riddle) comprises a wide variety of genres: parable, similitude, allegory, fable, proverb, apocalyptic revelation, riddle, symbol, pseudonym, fictitious person, example (model), theme, argument, apology, refutation, jest".[17] We don't need to worry too much about the difference between similitude and pseudonym: the key point here is that parables were much richer than single-point allegories. We might want to think of them as simple stories that conveyed complex messages.

Parables are not crossword puzzles that need to be solved and yet we often treat them as if they had been designed to catch us out. A better way of looking at them is as stories that yield their riches the more they are read. The world

17 Ratzinger, *Jesus of Nazareth*, 185.

is not straightforward and we are not straightforward, so parables provide a way in to the central mysteries of life. The importance of mystery in the Christian faith can hardly be exaggerated but it is often misunderstood. St Paul reminded the Romans that God "is able to strengthen you according to my gospel and the proclamation of Jesus Christ, according to the revelation of the mystery that was kept secret for long ages but is now disclosed" (Romans 16:25-26). He wrote to the Colossians about "the mystery that has been hidden throughout the ages and generations but has now been revealed to his saints" (Colossians 1:26). And he wrote to Timothy about "the mystery of the faith" (1 Timothy 3:9). "Mystery" was clearly an important concept for him; the difficulty we face is that it is a word that has become very debased. We tend to think that a mystery needs to be solved, whereas St Paul was clearly referring to something wonderful that had already been revealed or disclosed. Kallistos Ware explains the word in this way:

> In the proper religious sense of the term, "mystery" signifies not only hiddenness but disclosure. The Greek noun *mysterion* is linked with the verb *myein*, meaning "to close the eyes or mouth." The candidate for initiation into certain of the pagan mystery religions was first blindfolded and led through a maze of passages; then suddenly his eyes were uncovered and he saw, displayed all round him, the secret emblems of the cult. So, in the Christian context, we do not mean by a "mystery" merely that which is baffling and mysterious, an enigma or insoluble problem. A mystery is, on the contrary, something that is revealed for our understanding, but which we

> never understand exhaustively because it leads into the depths or darkness of God.[18]

That is why Flannery O'Connor was so keen on St Gregory of Nyssa's aphorism that "every time the sacred text describes a fact, it reveals a mystery". She wasn't arguing that the plain words of scripture lead us into obscurities that need explaining. Rather, she was suggesting that the word of God leads us towards the multifaceted wonders of God himself. All of which brings us back to the parables and Jesus as storyteller. It brings us back to Jesus who "told the crowds all these things in parables; without a parable he told them nothing. This was to fulfil what had been spoken through the prophet:

> 'I will open my mouth to speak in parables;
> I will proclaim what has been hidden from the foundation of the world.'"
>
> Matthew 13:34-35

It brings us back to Jesus who said, "... there is nothing hidden, except to be disclosed; nor is anything secret, except to come to light" (Mark 4:22) and who prayed, "I thank you, Father, Lord of heaven and earth, because you have hidden these things from the wise and the intelligent and have revealed them to infants" (Matthew 11:25). For Jesus, the parables were a way of revealing the mysteries of God to his people.

We sometimes speak about teaching as though it is merely the imparting of knowledge – the teacher's job being to tell students what they don't yet know – but there is a great deal

18 Kallistos Ware, *The Orthodox Way* (Crestwood, NY: St Vladimir's Seminary Press, 1995), 15.

more to teaching than delivering facts, as though the teacher were simply a conveyor belt of pre-packaged information. At its best, teaching leads students into a new way of living. The teacher teaches by example as well as with words, and students learn as all apprentices learn: by working alongside their teachers, by observing them, listening to them and following in their footsteps.

This is the message that the two disciples eventually understood while travelling on the road to Emmaus. When Jesus appeared on the road, he listened to them as they expressed their confusion, and then, "beginning with Moses and all the prophets, he interpreted to them the things *about himself* in all the scriptures" (Luke 24:27). What Jesus had to teach was himself. What Jesus had to give was himself. What he taught was ultimately not truths but the Truth himself. That is why, as the Fathers of Vatican II explained so beautifully, it is also true that "man... cannot fully find himself except through a sincere gift of himself".[19]

Let the little children come to me

It is in this pedagogical context that we can read the many references to children and childhood in the New Testament. It is in this context that St Louis de Montfort's astonishing claim about Jesus' submission to his mother makes sense: "Jesus Christ gave more glory to God the Father by submission to His Mother during those thirty years [before his public ministry began] than He would have given Him in converting the whole world by the working of the most stupendous miracles."[20]

19 Second Vatican Council, *Gaudium et Spes* (Pastoral Constitution on the Church in the Modern World), 24.
20 St Louis de Montfort, *True Devotion to Mary* (Rockford, IL: Tan Books, 1985), 18.

When the disciples rebuked the crowds for bringing their children to Jesus, Jesus "was indignant and said to them, 'Let the little children come to me; do not stop them; for it is to such as these that the kingdom of God belongs. Truly I tell you, whoever does not receive the kingdom of God as a little child will never enter it.' And he took them up in his arms, laid his hands on them, and blessed them" (Mark 10:14-16). This is such a familiar passage that we can miss how revolutionary Jesus' teaching was. He wasn't simply welcoming children into the group, he was providing a model for us all to follow. He was showing us how to make a sincere gift of ourselves by becoming like little children.

That is also why he called a child when the disciples asked him who was the greatest in the kingdom of heaven, telling them that "unless you change and become like children, you will never enter the kingdom of heaven. Whoever becomes humble like this child is the greatest in the kingdom of heaven. Whoever welcomes one such child in my name welcomes me" (Matthew 18:3-5). As adults, we believe that we can be self-sufficient: as children, we know that we are dependent. Children see clearly, while we may be blinded by our own superficial successes. What we see on earth is only a tiny fragment of a very great mosaic that is completed in heaven and yet how often we try to impress God with our work, our understanding and our adult ways. How often we try to convince ourselves that we see the whole picture, forgetting that it is the "little ones" whose "angels continually see the face of my Father in heaven" (Matthew 18:10).

Time and again in the Gospels, we see that Jesus wants us to appear before him like little children. To feed the five thousand, Jesus accepted five loaves and two fish from a child. To show that the kingdom of God had come, he healed not just adults but children too. To make it absolutely clear that he could overcome death, he brought not just Lazarus back from the dead but Jairus' daughter as well.

Children were at the heart of the Gospel, even when there wasn't a child in sight. At the Last Supper, Jesus called his disciples "little children" (John 13:33). After his resurrection, he called out to ask if his "children" had caught any fish when the disciples were fishing on the Sea of Tiberias (John 21:5). When he spoke about his love for the people of Jerusalem he said, "How often have I desired to gather your children together as a hen gathers her brood under her wings, and you were not willing!" (Luke 13:34).

We should draw huge encouragement from these passages. What Jesus asks of us is not examination success – not even religious studies examination success – but the humility of little children. What Jesus the teacher expects is not results but a willingness to learn. What Jesus gives is what he also wants from us: his very self. That is why he was the greatest teacher of all. Not because he taught a new philosophy or developed a new school of thought or introduced a new teaching style, but because he gave himself fully for us. What he expects is the same in return.

Come to me, all you that are weary and are carrying heavy burdens, and I will give you rest. Take my yoke upon you, and learn from me; for I am gentle and humble in heart, and you will find rest for your souls. For my yoke is easy, and my burden is light. Matthew 11:28-30

You have heard that it was said, "You shall love your neighbour and hate your enemy." But I say to you, Love your enemies and pray for those who persecute you, so that you may be children of your Father in heaven. Matthew 5:43-45

What can Jesus teach us about education today?

So what does all this mean for us today? Should we give up on the idea of school altogether and seek out the nearest range of mountains to abandon ourselves to God? I suppose that might be an option for a small number of people, but most of us are called to live out the life God has chosen for us exactly where we are now, in the circumstances in which we find ourselves now. That doesn't mean that we should always accept the status quo – we should always strive for growth in our schools, our families and our own lives – but it does mean that we shouldn't neglect the life that God has actually given us.

Living the life that God has given us and making a sincere gift of ourselves may seem extremely difficult, but if God wants our selves rather than our successes then we can let go of all the usual expectations that plague us. If God wants our children – and wants the best for our children – then we can also let go of the usual worries that afflict us as parents too, the sort of worries that French philosopher Gilles Lipovetsky writes about in one of his books:

> These days, young people start to become anxious about their choice of studies and the job those studies might lead to at a very early age. The Damocles sword of unemployment is impelling students to opt for prolonged courses of study, and to engage in a race for qualifications that are considered an insurance for the future. Parents too have taken on board the threats linked to hypermodern deregulation… it is

> training for the future that comes first; hence the vice, in particular, of educational consumerism, private lessons, and non-basic activities outside school.[21]

For Lipovetsky, our hypermodern age is one that is afflicted by deep-seated anxiety. Living in a consumer culture, we fend off the darkness by trying to buy our way into happiness, and when that doesn't work we become crippled by anxiety and foist that same anxiety onto our children. At those times we have to remind ourselves of Jesus' words in the Sermon on the Mount:

> [D]o not worry about your life, what you will eat or what you will drink, or about your body, what you will wear. Is not life more than food, and the body more than clothing? Look at the birds of the air; they neither sow nor reap nor gather into barns, and yet your heavenly Father feeds them. Are you not of more value than they? **Matthew 6:25-26**

Or, to bring the topic back to education, we need not worry about school results but should "strive first for the kingdom of God and his righteousness" (Matthew 6:33).

If anything, we need to extend our ambitions rather than limit them to mere examination success. As parents, our horizons should stretch far beyond public exam results. If we want the best for our children, our eyes should be firmly set on

21 Gilles Lipovetsky, *Hypermodern Times* (Cambridge: Polity Press, 2005), 46.

the furthest horizon of all because we want them to become saints. When Pope Benedict XVI spoke to schoolchildren during his visit to Britain in 2010, he expressed the hope that "among those of you listening to me today there are some of the future saints of the twenty-first century", explaining further that when he invited his young audience "to become saints, I am asking you not to be content with second best. I am asking you not to pursue one limited goal and ignore all the others".[22] Pursuing one limited goal and ignoring all the others is a temptation we are all prone to. Even if we manage to shed our own ambitions, we may still think that our children need to grow up with worldly success of some kind or another, even if that simply amounts to a good range of qualifications, a secure job and a house of their own. Without denying legitimate this-worldly aspirations, Pope Benedict suggested that we should have greater and higher ambitions:

> Having money makes it possible to be generous and to do good in the world, but on its own, it is not enough to make us happy. Being highly skilled in some activity or profession is good, but it will not satisfy us unless we aim for something greater still. It might make us famous, but it will not make us happy. Happiness is something we all want, but one of the great tragedies in this world is that so many people never find it, because they look for it in the wrong places. The key to it is very simple – true happiness is

22 Benedict XVI, "Address of the Holy Father to Pupils", Vatican Website (17 September 2010). https://w2.vatican.va/content/benedict-xvi/en/speeches/2010/september/documents/hf_ben-xvi_spe_20100917_mondo-educ.html#ADDRESS_OF_THE_HOLY_FATHER_TO_PUPILS., accessed 23 Oct. 2017.

> to be found in God. We need to have the courage to place our deepest hopes in God alone, not in money, in a career, in worldly success, or in our relationships with others, but in God. Only he can satisfy the deepest needs of our hearts.[23]

What we should want for ourselves, for our children and for our students is that the deepest needs of their hearts are satisfied. We should long for a life fully lived: not a life packed full with so-called peak experiences, but a life that resonates with the fullness and joy that can come only from God himself.

Education today

So what might this mean in practical terms? What can Jesus teach us about the nuts and bolts of education today?[24] A good place to start might be with Jesus as teacher of the scriptures. Fishermen and tax collectors his disciples may have been, but when he spoke, he repeatedly drew on the scriptures to explain what was required of them. It is clear that he could assume a high level of scriptural knowledge among his disciples, the words he used to introduce many of his points giving us a clear indication of the context in which his audience learned the word of God: "You have heard that it was said..." For many of those listening to the Sermon on the Mount, knowledge of the Bible came through the ears. They heard it in the synagogue and they knew it well. When Jesus spoke to the Pharisees, by contrast, he often

23 Benedict XVI, "Address of the Holy Father to Pupils".
24 I explore some of these ideas in more detail in *Out of the Classroom and Into the World: how to transform Catholic education* (New York: Angelico Press, 2018).

introduced his point by asking, "Have you never read..." The written word was also important, though not for everyone.[25]

Our teaching context is very different. We live in a culture that is primarily visual rather than aural, and there are very few people who know their Bibles in anything more than a cursory way. We are sometimes told that the answer to scriptural illiteracy is better religious education in schools. However, changing religious education lessons will only get us so far, partly because RE teachers have only a limited amount of time and partly because the culture is working against them. So what can be done?

If we want to make fundamental changes to our children's lives we must remember that, as parents, we are their primary educators. The answer to our children's educational difficulties starts with us. We may bemoan the state of the education in our schools, we may wish the level of catechesis was better in our parish churches, we may be disturbed by the amount of time our children spend looking at screens, but the answer starts with us. If we read the Bible there is a much greater chance that our children will follow suit.

Jesus' life and the lives of his disciples were permeated by the scriptures. We live in a different age, so we need to find different ways of providing that same scriptural context for our children's lives. Children's Bibles are useful up to a point – they provide our children with a good knowledge of the main biblical stories – but there is nothing to match the actual words of scripture. That is why Jean-François Kieffer's illustrated books are so good.[26] They are beautifully drawn but also stick closely to the original. That is also one reason why the Catechesis of the Good Shepherd makes such a

25 Alan Millard, *Reading and Writing in the Time of Jesus* (Sheffield: Sheffield Academic Press, 2001), 158.

26 See, for example, Jean-François Kieffer, *The Illustrated Gospel for Children* (San Francisco: Ignatius Press, 2010).

powerful impact on the children who experience it.[27] Sofia Cavalletti, who created the catechesis having worked with Maria Montessori, realised that children need to learn in a way that is appropriate for their age. She also understood the importance of the body and of learning through doing, so the Catechesis of the Good Shepherd is strikingly hands-on. Children move from "work" to "work" – to use Cavalletti's term – making and moving as they go, but every part of their catechesis is rooted in the actual words of scripture. It is so easy to assume that we need to retell Bible stories to children to make them accessible, but Jesus' parables – to give just one example – are accessible to everyone. We don't need to water down the Bible for it to make an impact.

Lectio divina in schools

Nonetheless, we do need to recognise that children grow up, so we have to be ready for the challenges that come when our children outgrow their children's Bibles and when illustrated editions no longer hold their attention. Needing to respect their growing maturity, we can also be confident that the Bible grows with them, being a pool deep enough for elephants to bathe in and shallow enough for mice to paddle in. There is no reason why children of secondary-school age, for example, cannot engage in *lectio divina*, as a wonderful group of Christians from Chile have convincingly shown. The Manquehue Apostolic Movement was started by José Manuel Eguiguren Guzman, who went through a deep spiritual crisis while he was at university in the 1970s. In that sense, he was not at all unusual. What *was* unusual was his response to that crisis. Meeting a Benedictine monk called Fr Gabriel Guarda from the Holy Trinity Monastery in Las Condes, José Manuel plucked up the courage to climb the hill to the monastery to seek his advice. To his great surprise,

27 See www.cgsuk.org for more details.

Fr Gabriel's response to José Manuel's many questions was not a series of answers but a book: he suggested that they pray to the Holy Spirit and turn to the Bible.

Day after day as he listened to José Manuel's anguished questions, Fr Gabriel's response was always the same: he suggested Bible passages they could read together and let the scriptures do their work. What José Manuel discovered was that the word of God was not a dead object to be subjected to scrutiny but a living word that searched him out. He came to the monastery with questions and eventually he discovered that it was the Bible that was questioning him. It is no exaggeration to say that *lectio divina* changed José Manuel's life, though it did not do so overnight. He went to see Fr Gabriel in the monastery at Las Condes almost every day for three years! You won't find many clearer examples of patience and perseverance than that.

Lectio divina changed José Manuel's life and it also changed many other people's lives as a consequence. Transformed by his experiences over three years, José Manuel found a new purpose for his life, initially by taking a confirmation class for eighteen-year-olds at his former school. Struggling to find a way to engage with the students, he decided to share with them what he had learned himself through *lectio divina* and watched in amazement as the word of God transformed their lives too. By the end of the process it was clear that a new path had emerged, so eight of the group joined with José Manuel in setting up the Manquehue Movement, which dedicated itself to creating a cloister in the world.[28] Inspired by the Benedictine tradition, they were also determined to live out their vocation as laymen in the world, bringing the word of God to schoolchildren in particular and encouraging them to share that same word of God with their peers.

28 Patrick Barry, *A Cloister in the World* (St Louis, MO: Outskirts Press, 2005).

Forty years later, the movement now has three schools in Chile and has also made a significant impact in the UK, as its members have worked with students in Benedictine schools across the country. Drawing on the example of the Liturgy of the Hours, José Manuel wanted the school day to be punctuated by prayer and prayerful reading of the Bible. "We always read one of the daily mass readings before classes and other important meetings or activities of the day," José Manuel wrote. "This repetition of the Gospel throughout the working day acts like a drop of water falling on stone, slowly marking a channel and forging a path to the depths of the heart."[29]

Another crucial aspect of the Manquehue Movement schools are *tutorías*, which are opportunities for older students to lead groups of younger students in *lectio divina*, in much the same way that St Philip helped the Ethiopian in the desert. In leading these groups, the older students are not teaching but are instead acting as spiritual companions to students who are just beginning on their journey of biblical exploration, standing alongside them in friendship as they learn to listen to what the Word of God has to say to each one of them through the word of God.

Spiritual companionship can take many forms. As St John Bosco showed many years ago, what happens out of lessons is often as important – if not more important – in this regard as what happens in them. Spending time with students at break or lunchtime is a crucial way of helping them to flourish. In the school where I currently work, each teacher has a small number of personal tutees with whom he or she meets once every two weeks. These meetings supplement the regular daily form tutor time and are an essential way of allowing teachers to get to know a small number of students

29 José Manuel Eguiguren, *Waking Up to God* (Stratton-on-the-Fosse: Downside Abbey Press, 2017), 285-286.

really well over time. So important are these tutorials that they can even take place during lesson time if necessary, though they are usually scheduled for break and lunchtime. If we want to draw on the example that Jesus gave when he taught his disciples, relying on form groups is never going to be enough to give our students what they really need. Knowing our sheep by name and being prepared to rescue them when they are lost is what is expected of us.

Spiritual friendship and education

The work of the Manquehue Movement suggests that we do not have to create new techniques to engage youngsters. Rather, we need to draw from the deep well of the scriptures so they can drink from the same living waters that have slaked the thirst of countless saints before them. We need to be confident that the Word of God – using the word of God – can still transform lives. We may need to change our educational priorities, focusing less single-mindedly on examination success and more explicitly on spiritual companionship and spiritual friendship, but that should not be an insuperable problem, especially if we are prepared to be inspired by treasures of Catholic tradition, such as the Rule of St Benedict and St Aelred's little book on *Spiritual Friendship*, as the Manquehue Movement is.

At the heart of Jesus' teaching was the time he spent with his disciples: three years living in very close proximity with the people he had chosen to lead his Church. Having spent thirty years in the Holy Family in Nazareth, Jesus lived out his public ministry in the company of men and women who gradually grew closer to their teacher as they became part of the new family of God. One way of describing our contemporary education system, by contrast, is as a gradual withdrawal of teachers from students. Teachers of four- to seven-year-olds spend a huge amount of time with their pupils. They may teach large classes but they still have a fair chance of getting to know their charges in a way that seems almost inconceivable to teachers further along the supply chain. As children become older, the demand for subject specialisation has an inevitable impact on the amount of time they get to spend with each of their teachers. This may, on occasion, be a relief to both teachers and children, but there are definite drawbacks. The less teachers see of their students, the less likely they are to get to know them. The less they see of them, the more likely they are to deliver information from arm's length and then move on. By the time students leave school and go to university, there is even less likelihood of their having meaningful interaction with their teachers over any extended period of time. The amount of contact time – to use that ugly piece of educational jargon – that students get varies enormously from subject to subject and from university to university, but, wherever they end up studying, students will certainly not receive the same amount of personal attention they had when they were five years old or that Jesus' disciples had when they were grown men.

Clearly there are economic factors at work here. It would be simply unaffordable for universities to give students the amount of contact time that Jesus gave to his disciples. Yet money is clearly not the only issue. A much higher level of involvement is deemed necessary for some courses, such as medicine, and some universities, such as Cambridge and Oxford, pride themselves on having a tutorial system that ensures a greater degree of interaction between teachers and students. Nonetheless, it is still entirely possible to spend the overwhelming majority of your time as an Oxbridge student working under your own steam.

It is also true that the school–university–career model on which the preceding analysis has been based is only one of several possible educational models. As I have suggested elsewhere in the book, the apprenticeship model fits much more closely with the kind of education Jesus gave his disciples. Working and learning alongside the teacher over an extended period of time works well for apprentices and for many businesses. That is why many school-leaver programmes implicitly follow the apprenticeship model even if they choose different language to describe their schemes.

If we want to learn from Jesus' example, we may soon come to accept that who the teacher is is far more important than what he or she teaches. As we have already seen, when Jesus was travelling on the road to Emmaus, "he interpreted to them the things about himself in all the scriptures" (Luke 24:27). The inevitable corollary is that managers should prioritise the recruitment of teachers whose lives are an example to their students, which is not an easy task in our current educational framework. If the person of the teacher really matters, and if, following the example of Jesus and St Joseph, we accept that apprenticeships provide the model to which all other courses should aspire, we also ought to ensure that teachers where possible are practitioners. We take it for granted that music teachers should play a musical instrument and that art teachers should be able to paint, sculpt and draw, but surely the same logic should apply to teachers of other subjects. History teachers should be researchers, scientists should carry out experiments and RE teachers should practise their faith. What's more, our students should see us doing this work and should learn alongside us while we are doing it. Such a claim may seem uncontroversial but you might be surprised how many English teachers claim they simply don't have time to read, let alone write. Through sheer busyness teachers can find that the subjects they love have become private passions to be enjoyed outside the school environment or, worse still, passions that have withered away altogether.

Time for education: time in education

Both *lectio divina* and spiritual friendship require time – instant results are simply not possible – which is why we need to learn to wait. Neither love nor education can be rushed. As parents, we have to wait for our children to become the people God wants them to be: we cannot expect the slow processes of physical and spiritual growth to speed up suddenly. We may try academic or religious hothousing but, whatever the short-term gains, we will find that the long-term results are disappointing. Much the same is true in our schools, where we can also be impatient for results, forgetting that children need to be nurtured over time and forgetting too that Jesus did not begin his public ministry until the age of thirty.

Unfortunately, the tendency in recent educational praxis has been to focus on short-term measures and so-called quick wins. Teachers are meant to have clear learning objectives for each class and are often obliged to find evidence that these objectives have been met by the end of the lesson. They are obliged to have schemes of work and dare not fall behind with the agreed pace of delivery. They are supposed to mould their students into some sort of final product – as though they were cars on an assembly line – by the time they reach the age of eighteen. The truth is that all these time frames are highly artificial. Learning does not take place in forty-five-minute chunks. The human brain does not operate according to a schedule set by school terms. And students don't stop growing the moment they pass through the school gate for the last time.

We can easily fall into the trap of believing that how schools operate now is how education has to be, but we only have to look back as far as pre-Reformation Europe to see that a different set of assumptions were at play. As educationalist David Hamilton explains, "[T]he sequence, length and completeness of medieval courses had been relatively open to student negotiation".[30] Degrees did not last three years. Programmes of study were not fixed. Lifelong learning was the norm. We don't need to become experts in educational history, however, to see that another way is possible. By looking at how Jesus taught, we can discover the vital importance of slow development over time. It is striking, for instance, that Jesus did not launch into a lesson on prayer straight after choosing his disciples: he waited until they asked him before teaching them the Our Father. The disciples had to see Jesus praying – and see the effects of prayer in his life – before they could develop the desire to pray in the same way. Having developed the desire they could then ask to be taught; having developed the desire they became capable of receiving the teaching that Jesus was always ready to give them.

Discipleship cannot be rushed. If God was prepared to wait for thousands of years until the people of Israel were ready to receive him, then we should be prepared to wait too. If Jesus was prepared to wait for thirty years before beginning his public ministry, then we should not assume that our children and students will develop any more quickly. If the disciples had to spend three years living with their master in order to learn from him, then we too should accept that we need time to become true disciples. Time matters in education, which is one reason why it is so important that we emphasise the importance of parents as primary educators. They are able to give their children what no school can ever match: their time and their love.

Time matters in education, whether that education takes place in the home or in school, but time for Christians is a complex concept. The Bible speaks of both *chronos*, ordered time, and *kairos*, the right time. When the devil

30 David Hamilton, *Towards a Theory of Schooling* (Barcombe: The Falmer Press, 1989), 45.

tempted Jesus in the desert, he "led him up and showed him in an instant [*chronos*] all the kingdoms of the world" (Luke 4:5), but when Jesus spoke about the end times, he told his disciples to "keep alert; for you do not know when the time [*kairos*] will come" (Mark 13:33).

The entry of Christ into the world of time changed time forever, as French historian François Hartog explained:

> As regards relations to time, Christianity's specific contribution was the decisive event of the Incarnation – the birth, death, and resurrection of the Son of God made man – which broke time in two. A new time started, which was to end with a second and last event, the Second Coming of Christ and the Last Judgment. The in-between time was a time of anticipation: a present inhabited by the promise of the end.[31]

It is this present inhabited by the promise of the end in which we now live. That is why we ask Our Lady to "pray for us sinners now and at the hour of our death". That is why we can be bold enough to ask our Father in heaven to "give us this day our daily bread". Waiting is difficult for all of us. It is hard to wait when the difficulties of family life become overwhelming. It is difficult to wait when change seems slow at school. We can all give way to impatience, knowing no other way to cope with the frustrations of life. In those situations we need to remember the advice of great spiritual writers who have gone before us, encouraging us to

31 François Hartog, *Regimes of Historicity: presentism and experiences of time* (New York: Columbia University Press, 2015), 60-61.

practise the presence of God and to accept the sacrament of the present moment.[32] We need to take our eyes off the future – because even the future will be ended in God – and look for God's grace in the present moment. "Do not be anxious about tomorrow," Jesus told his disciples, "for tomorrow will be anxious for itself. Let the day's own trouble be sufficient for the day" (Matthew 6:34). And he said that because God was with them – Jesus was with them – in the troubles of each day, and he was more than capable of carrying them through. His yoke was easy and his burden light. When we give ourselves to God in the present moment, we can bear all things, believe all things, hope all things and endure all things (1 Corinthians 13:7) because we know that he has already conquered sin and death in the past and that he will be coming again in the future. We know that the present moment belongs to him and that it is in the present moment that we will find him.

32 Brother Lawrence, *The Practice of the Presence of God* (London: Hodder & Stoughton, 2009); Jean-Pierre de Caussade, *The Sacrament of the Present Moment* (London: Fount, 1981).

In those days a decree went out from Emperor Augustus that all the world should be registered. This was the first registration and was taken while Quirinius was governor of Syria. All went to their own towns to be registered. Joseph also went from the town of Nazareth in Galilee to Judea, to the city of David called Bethlehem, because he was descended from the house and family of David. He went to be registered with Mary, to whom he was engaged and who was expecting a child. While they were there, the time came for her to deliver her child. And she gave birth to her firstborn son and wrapped him in bands of cloth, and laid him in a manger, because there was no place for them in the inn. Luke 2:1-7

Epilogue

Parents, children and education: three questions or one?

It is Christmas. We have been to Mass, the turkey has been eaten and the presents have been unwrapped. My younger daughter is playing with playdough and my elder is growing crystals from her new chemistry set. Is this education or entertainment? And who is having more fun: the children or the parents? The answer to both questions is "both". We are making playdough ice creams together and together we are trying to work out the best way of growing crystals. For the purposes of this book, I have created separate sections on parents, children and education, but the truth is that they always belong together. As the Christmas Octave unfolds this becomes ever more apparent, the Feast of the Holy Family in particular suggesting that parents, children and education are inseparable, though it is also true that the Christmas season reminds us that, of the three, children are the most important.

There is another present sitting in a box that we are looking forward to playing as a family: *The Road to Bethlehem* game. The idea, in a nutshell, is that we have to make our way to see the Holy Family, overcoming any obstacles that get in our way as we travel. It is an idea that has already been played out in one way or another throughout Advent. As Mary and Joseph travelled, we travelled with them, preparing our hearts to receive the Christ child as they prepared to receive him into their family. The nature of that journey will have differed for each one of us, but what never changes is the necessity of the journey itself. None of us has arrived yet: we are all still on our pilgrimage of faith.

So maybe it is worth finishing this brief book about parents, children and education by prayerfully rereading Luke's account of the journey to Bethlehem and the nativity of Our Lord. What God wants to say to each one of us through this passage may well vary enormously, but what strikes me about the passage is how understated it is. If a novelist were to tell the story, he or she would probably make a great deal of the impact that politics had on everyday life, of the anguish the heavily pregnant woman felt at having to make such a journey, and of the dangerous humiliation that was visited upon the family when they were turned away from the inn. Luke, by contrast, packs an enormous emotional punch by stating the facts in an unadorned manner: "And she gave birth to her firstborn son and wrapped him in bands of cloth, and laid him in a manger, because there was no place for them in the inn." The facts speak for themselves. The simplicity of the account demands a response from us.

However complicated our own lives are, our difficulties don't come anywhere near the ones faced by the Holy Family, and however messy our lives become, the answer to our problems doesn't change from the one that was given two thousand years ago. A child has been born. The answer has already been spoken. God has already given us his Word.

The birth of Christ is the reason we can live with confidence in the present moment. That doesn't mean that the messiness of life is instantly cleared up or that we can abandon our journey. God has already spoken definitively in his Son, but our pilgrimage goes on. Yet, with the end in sight and the path already made straight, we can move forwards with great determination. And we should never forget that we are not travelling alone. Just like the disciples on the road to Emmaus, it gradually dawns on us that Jesus is already there when all seems lost. He has gone ahead of us and he is still with us. In this great mystery of faith, we can find all the strength we need to continue.

That is why, in the end, questions about parents, children and education are not three questions but one. What we tend to separate always comes together in Christ. Fallen humanity splits parents from children, school from home, what we learn in class from the rich wholeness of life. But in the one God – in the great unity of Father, Son and Holy Spirit – everything comes together. What we separate becomes whole once more.